EXCELLENCE IN MINISTRY

Best Practices for Successful Catechetical Leadership

TOM QUINLAN

THE EFFECTIVE CATECHETICAL LEADER

Series Editor Joe Paprocki, DMin

LOYOLA PRESS.
A JESUIT MINISTRY
Chicago

LOYOLA PRESS.
A JESUIT MINISTRY

3441 N. Ashland Avenue
Chicago, Illinois 60657
(800) 621-1008
www.loyolapress.com

Unless otherwise indicated, Scripture quotations contained herein are from the New Revised Standard Version Bible: Catholic Edition, copyright © 1993 and 1989 by the Division of Christian Education of the National Council of the Churches of Christ in the U.S.A. Used by permission. All rights reserved.

Scripture quotations designated NABRE are from the New American Bible revised edition © 2008, 1991, 1986, 1970. Confraternity of Christian Doctrine, Inc., Washington DC. All Rights Reserved.

Cover art credit: Ann Triling/Hemera/Thinkstock.

ISBN: 978-0-8294-4532-9
Library of Congress Control Number: 2017948967

Printed in the United States of America.
17 18 19 20 21 22 23 24 25 26 27 Versa 10 9 8 7 6 5 4 3 2 1

Contents

Welcome to The Effective Catechetical Leader Series

The Effective Catechetical Leader series provides skills, strategies, and approaches to ensure success for leaders of parish faith-formation programs. It will benefit anyone working with catechists, including Directors of Religious Education, pastors, diocesan directors, and catechetical training programs. Combining theory and practice, this series will

- provide practical instruction and printable resources;
- define the role of the catechetical leader and offer specific and practical strategies for leading, collaborating, and delegating;
- offer approaches for leading and catechizing in a more evangelizing way; and
- describe best practices for recruiting, training, and forming catechists; developing a vision for faith formation; forming an advisory board; planning and calendaring; networking with colleagues; selecting quality catechetical resources; handling the administrative aspects of the ministry; and identifying various groups to be catechized and approaches that meet the unique needs of those various groups.

Whether you are starting out as a catechetical leader or have been serving as one for many years, **The Effective Catechetical Leader** series will help you use every aspect of this ministry to proclaim the gospel and invite people to discipleship.

About This Book

Catechetical leadership is at its best when it builds on the shoulders of those who have gone before while at the same time creating innovative approaches for an ever-changing ministry. This fifth volume of **The Effective Catechetical Leader Series** will share both time-tested and new skills and strategies that will allow catechetical leaders not only to be successful in the week-to-week particulars of running a parish catechetical program, but also to fulfill the ultimate goal of animating a faith community to grow in authentic discipleship to Jesus Christ. A few of the best practices covered in this book include planning the catechetical year, selecting catechetical resources, promoting the catechetical program to the parish community and beyond, honestly evaluating your program, and so much more.

1

Forming and Sharing the Vision

Catechetical Advisory Boards and Vision Statements

"No one of us is as smart as all of us." So said the late Bishop Roger Kaffer, auxiliary bishop in the Diocese of Joliet, with whom I had the privilege of serving. Bishop Kaffer was humble, holy, hardworking, joyful, and a bit quirky. He had many other memorable sayings. I called them "Kafferisms."

Bishop Kaffer was the secretary for education when I began my tenure as diocesan catechetical director in 2001. I had plenty to learn, and he provided great mentorship to me. He told me his war stories as principal of a Catholic high school and as rector of the diocesan seminary. They revealed a leadership style that was both decisive when necessary and inclusive whenever possible. He believed firmly in the principle of subsidiarity, which calls for decision making to be as grassroots as possible. But he wasn't afraid to make a tough call, too. Bishop Kaffer, in his many roles as priest, principal, and bishop, had the instinct to invite input from stakeholders and strive for a consensus. He understood that autocratic leadership might result in poor decision making and implementation.

Countless times since his death, I've heard the echo of his counsel, "No one of us is as smart as all of us." It is a comforting thought that I don't need to have all the answers. I can lead a ministry with conviction and determination. Indeed, I should. But the ministry I am called to lead is not my own. It is bigger than I. It is the ministry of a parish, a diocese, that of the Church and of Christ himself! Understanding that I am a temporary steward of a ministry of the Church positions me to serve with humility. In recognizing and activating the giftedness of others, I surrender control and open myself to richer grace and greater possibilities.

Asking the Right Questions

One of my favorite speakers and authors is Patrick Lencioni, a highly respected consultant to Fortune 500 companies, an engaging speaker, and a devout Catholic. His books and Web videos are entertaining and filled with down-to-earth insights that are applicable in both corporate settings and the Church world. Lencioni names six questions that any organization needs to answer. They are

- Why do we exist?
- How do we behave?
- What do we do?
- How will we succeed?
- What is most important—right now?
- Who must do what?
  (*The Advantage: Why Organizational Health Trumps Everything Else in Business*, p. 77)

These are powerful questions. Do you notice that they are "we" questions? They suggest that there is more than one person at the table. They imply that organizational health requires the participation of different voices. Many businesses fail to address these questions. Many parishes do as well. Perhaps it is because these parishes have never been challenged to look at the big picture. Perhaps it is because staff and stakeholders are simply too busy keeping the operations running (smoothly or not). Maybe it is because asking these questions would bring to the surface the uncomfortable realization that much of what we are doing lacks purpose and direction, often with ineffectual outcomes.

There's a story about a daughter asking her mother for direction on how to make a pot roast. Her mother tells her to start by cutting off the ends. "Why?" the daughter asks. "I don't know," replies the mother. "It's what your grandmother always did." Upon asking the grandmother, she replied, "Oh, I did that because our pot back then wasn't big enough to fit a full roast." When someone questions the status quo in your parish, does anyone say, "We've always done it this way" or "We tried something like that once and it didn't work"? Well, maybe it's time the parish got a bigger pot!

Your Ministry Role in the Larger Context

As a catechetical leader, be it in a large parish with a staff to supervise or as a volunteer in a small parish, you have been empowered and you have authority. You are the agent of the pastor, who is chief catechetical leader of the parish. The pastor is an agent of the bishop, who happens to be the chief catechetical leader for a diocese. You function within this structure of the Catholic Church, and your role comes with great responsibility. You are accountable for the healthy functioning of the ministries within your job description.

This might seem like a lot of pressure, especially if you don't feel that you have adequate training or education or experience for the job. Happily, we do not have to have all the wisdom ourselves (as dear Bishop Kaffer pointed out). We, as catechetical leaders, already have the mission of the Church as the foundation upon which we build, lead, and serve in the ministry entrusted to us.

The Evangelizing Mission

Pope Paul VI in his 1975 encyclical *Evangelii Nuntiandi* (*Evangelization in the Modern World*) names our mission: "Evangelizing is in fact the grace and vocation proper to the Church, her deepest identity. She exists in order to evangelize" (*EN*, #14). How simple; how powerful! It doesn't stop there, however! Just a few short years later (1979), Pope St. John Paul II explained that catechesis is a moment—"a very remarkable one—in the whole process of evangelization" (*Catechesi Tradendae*, #18). Your ministry, my ministry, the ministry of all empowered to lead and serve in the Catholic Church is grounded in the evangelical mission of Jesus Christ. As the Word Incarnate, Jesus came to proclaim the Good News—the word of divine truth, mercy, and salvation. We are servants and echoers of this word. (The term *catechesis* means "echo.") The job you have been commissioned to do is ultimately grounded in proclaiming Jesus to the world so that all may come to know him and love him and become his disciples in the building of the reign of God here, and ultimately to attain eternal joy in heaven.

Wow! That is the mission we participate in, no matter how grand or humble our place may be in the Church. I hope it gives you a sense of meaning and purpose to be a part of something so beautiful and important. Nothing could be *more* important. With our universal mission understood, we can start to consider practical ways we can plan for success in our particular ministry.

Your Specific Ministry Leadership Role

You were hired for a particular position in a particular parish (or parishes). Given that each parish is different, you function in a unique ministry context. You could say that your job is as unique as a snowflake: no one else on earth has exactly *your* job. Take a close look at your job description. Is it clear to you what the job entails? What are the areas of parish life and ministry you oversee?

To whom do you report? Do you supervise others? Who are your team members?

If you don't have a job description, you should begin to build one in consultation with others, starting with your pastor and/or immediate supervisor. For more detail on formulating a role description, see book 1 of this series, *Called By Name*. Once you have an understanding of your responsibilities, you are in a position to begin to imagine building and strengthening the ministries you manage. Your vision and expertise are blessings. Your energy and passion are from God, who has seen fit to put you in this role.

Remembering that "no one of us is as smart as all of us," you will want to utilize the broader wisdom of the parish community for consultation and engagement. This consultation can come to you informally, by means of your expressed and implicit openness to input from all stakeholders. Every conversation is an opportunity to hear how things are going and to gain insight on how things might be improved. Listen well.

Stakeholders and Structures in the Parish

Your catechetical ministry does not take place within a vacuum. Every parish is the Body of Christ—a complex living organism with many moving parts. Stakeholders are those who have a concern or interest in a ministry or parish structure. They can impact it or be impacted by its actions. Not all stakeholders are equal. Here are examples of ministries and their stakeholders:

Religious Education Program Stakeholders	Adult Formation/ Evangelization Stakeholders
Pastor and staff	Pastor and staff
Children and parents	Parishioners being served directly
Catechists and others in support roles	Parishioners not being served
Parishioners	Nonparishioners

Some of these "moving parts" in the parish are actually formal channels built into the structure of the parish, such as the parish pastoral council. Often, a more localized consultative group—a catechetical advisory board—exists to serve the catechetical leader(s) of a parish, with a more particular focus on faith-formation ministry. You may have inherited such a group when taking your position. If an advisory board does not exist, I strongly encourage you to create one; I explain more about this in the chapter.

Leadership Structure for Catechetical Ministry

Let's look at the example of a religious-education advisory board. (Religious education, or RE, for reference in this book implies children's faith-formation ministry.) It may also be called a "child faith-formation committee" or other title, depending on factors particular to the parish. In most cases, such a board or committee will feed into a broader faith-formation commission that relates more directly to the parish pastoral council. (It is often at the commission level that parish RE and Catholic school will have shared representation, along with youth and adult formation. In this way a parish faith-formation commission can be valuable for creating a common vision for catechesis across the parish.)

Note the term *advisory*. Generally, a religious-education board serves to advise. This doesn't diminish its importance. To engage in dialogue and consultation can be extremely valuable and should be given full consideration. However, parish executive decisions (that *execute* a plan) are typically made at the staff level by the pastor and his pastoral staff and not by this consultative body. Those coming onto an advisory board should understand and be comfortable with this.

A religious-education advisory board typically does some or all of the following functions:

- Participates in and encourages strategic planning (both long- and short-term)
- Reviews policy
- Provides financial oversight
- Evaluates programs
- Serves as a conduit between leadership and parish
- Participates on catechetical-leader search committees as required

The number of members on a religious-education board is not fixed. Based on group-work studies and the stakeholders to be represented, its size should range from six to ten members. As the director or coordinator of religious education, you will want to make sure that you have the primary stakeholders, namely parents and catechists, represented in such a group. Whether the parish school participates in this group or not will impact the representation on such a body.

What kind of people do we want to serve on such an advisory board? Members should

- be invested in the parish and the ministry in question;
- provide sufficient diversity to represent the stakeholders of the parish;
- bring an informed perspective and be willing to express their convictions;

- understand that they are serving the greater good of the ministry in question and not their own agenda;
- be able to faithfully attend meetings and do their prep work; and
- be willing to put in some work to help achieve the goals set for the ministry.

It is worth emphasizing that serving on any kind of board, committee, or commission requires a person to rise above his or her own needs and concerns. A catechetical leader should be conscious of this in the process of finding good candidates, with the appropriate mind-set, to participate on a board. Those who are narrow minded and agenda driven need not apply.

Do Boards Do *Work?*

In theory, advisory boards don't do the "work" of the ministry, per se. So, the last listed item could be optional. But from my years of serving parish catechetical leaders, I have frequently heard how valuable a board or committee can be in helping to get things done. However, you have to be careful and reasonable in how much to put on the plates of parents, who are often very busy themselves, and of catechists, who are already doing important ministry. If you ask too much of your board, you might not keep them very long and might have difficulty bringing good people on.

Therefore, be circumspect about how you *work* your board, if you choose to do so. Be attentive to their giftedness and their interests, for if their responsibilities are properly aligned to their gifts and interests, they will be happier and more effective.

Entering and Exiting an RE Board

There is no fixed approach for recruiting members to serve on a board. Many boards are entirely appointed by the catechetical leader (perhaps with input or approval from the pastor). Some boards have members discerned or elected from their ranks—of catechists, parents, and other possible groups. Some are a combination of these approaches. A term of two to three years, with possible renewal, allows for adequate continuity within the body while avoiding stagnation. Dismissal from a board can occur but may be disruptive. The hope is that a sound process of appointment and/or discernment will prevent the need from arising.

If you will be appointing or inviting people to join the board, consult with others for their knowledge and input, especially if you are relatively new to the position. Avoid stacking the deck with people who think as you do. A board is of little value to a leader when it is filled with "yes" people. Rather, look for good and talented people who bring a diversity of experience, perspectives, and expertise. Disagreement and even some conflict is healthy for any group. If your board is lacking in certain areas, such as technology or marketing, consider seeking out a good candidate who can bring such expertise to the group.

Creating a Vision

Before a board enters into the work of planning, advising, and taking on possible tasks, it should engage in "visioning" work. Visioning means stepping back from the specific issues that need attention ("Should we add an additional hall monitor?" or "Do we want to explore a different text series for junior high next year?"), and looking at things from ten thousand feet . . . or even thirty thousand feet!

Effective boards stay connected to the big picture of why religious-education ministry exists. (Look back and you'll see this is the first of Lencioni's important questions.) A board or commission should always be aware that the religious-education program (and the school and every other ministry) is an arm of the parish and ultimately serves mission fulfillment of the Church, from which all else flows. Understanding this larger context, a board or commission or council is now ready to prayerfully forge a vision statement for its ministry.

While a mission statement articulates *why* a business or institution exists in the present (for whom and for what benefit), a vision statement names its desired broad and future-oriented outcomes.

Mission Statement Example: St. Joseph Parish exists to evangelize, proclaiming Christ's Good News so that all may experience God's love and mercy and so the world may resemble the Kingdom of God.

Vision Statement Example: St. Joseph Parish Faith Formation will help families in its program fall in love with Jesus and each year more deeply experience his love through participation in

- catechetical offerings,
- service opportunities,
- family faith discussions, and
- engagement in the life of the parish, especially liturgy.

Vision statements seek to answer the following questions:

1. What do we want to do in the future? (project a few years into the future)
2. When will this happen?
3. How will this happen?

Following are a few more tips about formulating a vision statement:

- Your vision statement should be brief, specific, simple, measurable, and ambitious.
- Start by being very clear about what it is that the catechetical program "does," and then add your unique angle to the outcome you are articulating.
- Think of what needs to be changed, what problem(s) needs to be addressed, and why.

- While your vision statement should be ambitious, make sure it is not so lofty that it can never truly be achieved. In other words, describe what "success" will look like.

- Make sure it can be easily remembered and explained by all who are guided by it.

Imagine you are part of a large rowing team out at sea. If you are all rowing with a fixed point on the horizon as your destination reference, it becomes easier for the captain to get (and keep) the boat headed in the right direction. A vision statement can serve as that reference point for where this ministry needs to go.

Ongoing Formation for Advisory Board Members

Make high-quality prayer experiences a part of every advisory board meeting. (Chapter 8 considers this topic more.) Encourage your board to participate in ongoing formation that includes exploring theology, spirituality, and pedagogy, along with pertinent cultural topics (such as the digital media age and modern family dynamics). Weave special retreats and formation experiences into the rhythm of the year, both to enhance their service to the board and to bless them in their own right. Among the many ways to show appreciation to your trusted advisors is to help them grow in their knowledge of the Catholic faith and to experience the love of Christ in their own lives.

Summary: Go and Make Disciples

Go therefore and make disciples of all nations. (Matt. 28:19)

An organization with vision asks the right questions. As ministers of the Church, the question "Why do we exist?" has already been answered for us: to go and make disciples of all nations. The specifics of our vision as catechetical leaders must be worked out in each parish's particular context, but they should all (including your job description) be directed to this end and discerned in community. Relying on an advisory board shows that you are a catechetical leader who recognizes that "no one of us is as smart as all of us."

For Reflection and Discussion

- What are the gifts God has given you to use in serving your parish? What are some gifts you do not have that you should seek out in others to share in your ministry?

- Making disciples, especially of all nations, is something that requires teamwork and shared vision. Do you have an advisory body to help you? Do you truly value their insight and help, or do you primarily find yourself wishing you could "do it yourself"?

Growing as a Catechetical Leader

The *National Directory for Catechesis* reminds us that "every parish needs to develop a coherent catechetical plan that integrates the various components of the overall program and provides opportunities for all parishioners to hear the Gospel message, celebrate it in prayer and Liturgy, and live it in their daily lives" (#60A). As in the example of a rowing team's captain, do you have a sense of where you're steering your parish's catechetical ministry? How are you going to get there? What and who will help you to develop this sense more clearly?

Go to www.loyolapress.com/ECL to access the worksheet.

Suggested Action

Schedule some time this week to reflect on Patrick Lencioni's six questions (page 2) for your ministry. Then, think about the members on your existing advisory board (or whom you might invite to start a board) and the gifts/perspectives each one brings to the table. Next, come up with a simple plan for inviting your board to reflect on these same questions and share their insights.

For Further Consideration

The Advantage: Why Organizational Health Trumps Everything Else in Business. Patrick Lencioni (San Francisco: Jossey-Bass, 2012).

Fostering Leadership Skills in Ministry: A Parish Handbook. Jean Marie Hiesberger (Liguori, MO: Liguori Publications, 2012).

Mission and Vision Statement Workbook. Rev. Jessica Crane Munoz (CreateSpace Independent Publishing Platform, 2016).

National Directory for Catechesis. (Washington, DC: United States Conference of Catholic Bishops, 2005).

Vatican Council II: Constitutions, Decrees, Declarations. Austin Flannery, ed. (Northport, NY: Costello Publishing, 1996).

2

Planning and Evaluating
Catechetical Ministries

Planning to Be Spontaneous

Some of us are meticulous planners and some of us like to make it up as we go along. Which one better describes you? I say "*better* describes you" because few of us are completely at one extreme or the other. This is definitely the case for me.

After years of imagining an adventure and planning to take a long road trip and "make the journey the destination," I finally hit the road in the summer of 1999, not quite sure how it would all work. The plan was to be spontaneous (irony intended). For the next six months, I followed my quasi-itinerary. My assiduous planning efforts allowed me to be intuitive, free to listen to my gut a bit as the months went by and I had to make decisions about the trip. Having the flexibility to make course corrections as I went was built into the plan and gave me both clarity and freedom. (This journey also gave me the psychic space to creatively explore and discern God's call to make catechetical leadership my life's vocational work.)

From this example, you can see that I am somewhere between an utter control freak and a modern-day hippie. And the lesson here for catechetical leadership is, I believe, that you need both a plan and the flexibility to adjust as circumstances warrant. Good planning frees us rather than restricts us.

Planning and Constant Change

Far too many parishes and catechetical programs seem to run on autopilot. I call that "keeping the trains running on time." It might be excusable to function this way for a time when things are going well or if you are just beginning. But all too quickly inertia will start to creep in. Saint Ignatius is said to have remarked, "He who is not getting better is getting worse." Another way of putting it is, if we are standing still, the world will pass us by. Planning helps us to keep moving, we hope, in a coherent, reasoned direction.

Don't fear change. Rather, embrace it. Everything is changing all the time, whether we like it or not. The only place where we can escape change is the cemetery! To be engaged in great human endeavors, such as bringing God and people into relationship (the great catechetical endeavor), requires a degree of surrender and courageous openness to the inevitable *change* dynamic.

Don't feel daunted by the need to plan. Rather, be excited. You are not alone as you engage in planning with your pastor and staff colleagues, your board, and perhaps the parish pastoral council—also, catechetical leaders in other parishes. Planning will help to harness your knowledge, passion, and creativity as you build structure for what is to come. It will position your ministry for success.

Good planning factors in change that is already occurring and attempts to anticipate change still on the horizon. We are called to be leaders who are change agents and responsible planners—detail oriented and visionary, structured and flexible—seeing change as *opportunity* and not as the enemy.

The Gospels' Approach to Planning

What is Jesus' take on planning? At times Jesus teaches in a way that clearly espouses prudent planning. The parable of the Ten Brides-maids (Matt. 25:1–13) celebrates the five bridesmaids at a wedding who brought enough oil to last through the night, while chastising the ones who were unprepared. On the other hand, in the parable of the Rich Fool (Luke 12:13–21) Jesus condemns a landowner for think-ing he will secure his future by building bigger barns to fill with his abundance.

Perhaps the takeaway is that Jesus wants us to use the gifts of reason and foresight in service to our relationship with God and the build-ing of the reign of God. However, we must take care never to develop a sense of autonomy from the grace that sustains us or independence from the Holy Spirit who must direct our efforts.

Plan with the End in Mind

How cliché, and yet how true! Plan with the end in mind. And what is the end goal for catechetical ministry? Saint Pope John Paul II states it very concisely: "The definitive aim of catechesis is to put people not only in touch but in communion, in intimacy, with Jesus Christ" (*Cat-echesi Tradendae*, #5).

All of us in catechetical leadership are given a common mission and are charged with the challenge of discerning how to accomplish it within our particular role and unique context. This is the right starting place. Our Church gives us further direction upon which we should base our planning. The *General Directory for Catechesis (GDC)* and the *National Directory for Catechesis* are both seminal works for any-one in catechetical leadership. They should not only be on our shelves but also activated in our leadership. (These and other key catechetical documents are treated in depth in book 3 of the The Effective Cate-chetical Leader series, *Developing Disciples of Christ*.) In the *GDC* we find an important set of mandates for what our faith-formation ministry must achieve. They are called the "Six Tasks of Catechesis":

1. Knowledge of the faith
2. Liturgy and the sacraments
3. Moral formation
4. Prayer
5. Community life
6. Missionary initiation

These six facets of our ministry are important to keep before us as we plan for a ministry or program. Whether we oversee formation ministry of children, youth, or adults, whether we are involved with initiation ministry or special-needs faith formation, the Six Tasks of Catechesis serve as a framework within which to plan.

From Bigger to Smaller: Planning within Context

When it comes to planning, there is long-term planning, which might extend five years, and there is short-term planning, which looks out into the next year. Both have a place in catechetical ministry.

Long-term planning should be done with an eye to the vision of the diocese and of the parish. Check with your diocesan catechetical office for insight into your bishop's diocesan vision, priorities, and any particular initiatives on the horizon. As for your parish, the parish pastoral council should be developing and articulating an overarching vision and plan, in collaboration with your pastor. Be fully engaged in the conversation at the parish-staff level. An effective staff has regular meetings where the expertise of the staff members can engage the vision of the pastor and the parish pastoral council and translate the evangelizing mission of the Church into a long-term parish strategy.

Where is your parish headed? I like to say that a well-functioning parish walks on two legs, that of its leadership structure (pastoral council and commissions) and its pastoral staff. If one of these two legs is ailing, the parish limps. If one of the legs is immobilized, the parish goes in circles. For a parish to actually go somewhere significant, both its leadership structure and staff must be not only in motion but also in *coordinated* motion. Thus, it is vital that there are opportunities for interface between parish leadership structures and parish staff. It is here that dialogue can lead to trust and understanding, and constructive cross-pollination can take place.

The pastoral staff and the parish pastoral council each need to have a clear sense of the other's place and function. As a result of such collaboration, a broad sense of direction for the parish can be established that the staff can begin to implement. Here are some foundational elements for constructive parish catechetical planning.

- Be in sponge mode—listen and learn continually.
- Assemble a healthy faith-formation board (or committee or commission).
- Get a sense of who you are as a leader and how your style fits with the "culture" of the parish and the rest of the pastoral staff.
- Engage in big-picture discussion with parish leadership structures and staff.

Remember, faith-formation ministry is an element of the broader life of the parish. Staying properly aligned to the vision of the parish and its strategic direction is vitally important. Any catechetical vision and goals need to be in sync with that of the parish, or at least not be at counter purposes.

Some parishes have very small staffs, and others either have no leadership structures or the structures are ineffectual. If there happens to be a vacuum of parish direction and planning at your church, this means you have more of a blank canvas on which to paint a vision for faith-formation ministry. A greater responsibility rests on the planning you will conduct, and also a greater opportunity that perhaps your catechetical visioning and planning will serve as leaven for the larger parish dynamic. With these initial elements in place, let's look at catechetical planning in greater depth.

Understanding Planning Terms

We have already explored mission and vision in chapter 1. Now is a good time to discuss more specific components of planning, namely establishing goals, objectives, strategies, and tactics. For our purposes, let's define them.

- Goals
  - have a broad primary outcome
  - should be few in number, perhaps two to three goals at a time
- Objectives
  - are measurable steps toward accomplishing a goal
  - help to assess success
- Strategies
  - are methods for achieving an objective
- Tactics
  - are a set of specific activities that implement a strategy
  - are small, specific actions that can be numerous and varied

Case Study: Young Adult Ministry and Lenten Small Faith Groups— To help explain these terms as concepts within planning, here is an example of how this might work in a parish.

- *Goal*: To increase the engagement of young adults in faith formation
- *Objective*: Achieve a 25 percent increase in the participation of young adults in named areas (Lenten small faith groups, Theology-on-Tap series, mission experiences, etc.).
- *Strategy* (for Lenten small faith groups): More effective marketing
- *Tactics*: Earlier marketing, including mention in all Advent/Christmas communications
- Better marketing, including use of color, graphics, and photos
- Intensive marketing, utilizing all standard parish means but with greater frequency
- Targeted marketing through means that specifically reach young adults, including:
  - Putting up flyers in coffee shops, bars, and other young-adult venues
  - Getting mentions on local radio, in community newspaper
  - Using Facebook ads designed to attract young adults
  - Asking young-adult parishioners to invite friends, neighbors, and coworkers

Here again we are reminded to plan with the end in mind. In the above example, the end is not really just to get more young adults to show up for parish events and activities. The end, the mission that is to be served in this planning, is to foster deep and abiding conversion to Jesus Christ, in this case in young adults in the parish and beyond. The Lenten small-group faith ministry is a means to achieving the goal (to increase area young adult engagement)—a goal developed out of, and in service to, the Universal Church's mission.

Not only is the Lenten small-group faith ministry a means to this end, but so is the parish itself. We must remember that all institutional structures of the Church, including the parish, are not ends in themselves but means. It is a professional hazard of those of us who serve within the Church to sometimes lose sight of this. Any entity that functions as if its own perpetuation is the reason it exists is doomed to fail. Being mission driven is the key for any company or institution to thrive.

I often recall the words of a late friend and colleague, Russell Peterson: "I don't trust anyone who talks more about the Church than about Jesus." For the Catholic Church, the mission is Jesus Christ! Plan with this end in mind.

Ongoing monitoring is important when starting a program. A good idea is to post goals, objectives, strategies (and possibly tactics) somewhere prominently in your office to remind yourself to revisit them and monitor progress. Consider providing a comparable posting to other key members of the team. Ongoing progress should be a periodic item for team meetings. Celebrate progress, affirm effort, and hold one another accountable (charitably!) to keep things on course with regard to outcomes, timeline, and budget.

Don't Forget to Evaluate

Looking at the case study mentioned previously, let's focus on evaluating the Lenten small faith groups. If you have data on the age ranges of participants in this ministry from the year before and after this goal was created, the percentage change for young adult participation in the Lenten small faith group ministry can easily be calculated. This percentage change can then be compared to the objective set for growing young adult participation in the parish. Data can also reveal their attendance pattern at sessions over the course of Lent and provide other statistical measurements.

Along with hard data metrics, there are qualitative means for measuring the success of an effort. What comments were provided by young adults (in formal written feedback or anecdotally) about the faith-group experience? How would group leaders describe young adults' level of engagement during sessions? What number of young adults, if invited, accepted a role to lead a group next year? Did the parish engagement of young adult participants change, and how?

Some dioceses (such as the Dioceses of San Diego, California, and Lafayette, Indiana) provide evaluation instruments for parish catechetical programs, so be sure to contact your local catechetical office. Likewise, the National Catholic Education Association's *Information for Growth: Assessment of Children/Youth Religious Education* (IFG/ ACRE) is a helpful resource for evaluating a parish religious-education program. For more information, visit www.ncea.org.

Imagining Great Possibilities

It is important to enter any planning with a ready knowledge of the parameters and limitations in a parish setting. In the end, planning must be tethered to reality. However, don't start planning with all the limits and restrictions in front of you and the faith-formation board. Considering the state that many parishes find themselves in, doing so would leave most feeling hopeless.

Personally, I love *what-if* and *why-not* questions. I suggest starting the planning process with a sense of blue-sky possibilities rather than red-ink impossibilities. Maybe create a mini-retreat experience—a day when planning can be conducted in a relaxed atmosphere away from the parish and in the context of prayer. Such an experience would be conducive for imagining what *should* happen to serve the mission of the Church and the vision of the parish. Spend time in that hopeful and exciting place of possibility before too quickly pivoting to what *can* happen.

Holy Fire That Lights the Horizon

Hope is one of the greatest assets a parish can have. And I find all too often that parish leaders, beset by the weight of years of managing decline, have lost their ability to vision beyond the shrinking budget and decreasing parishioner count. Don't let that be you. Serve your parish well by fighting against a culture of despair and paralysis wherever you find it, whether on the staff, in leadership structures, or broadly among parishioners. Sometimes the flame of hope needs to be re-lit before any meaningful planning for the future can take place. You can be a fire starter.

Of course, the ultimate fire starter is the Holy Spirit. All visioning and planning must occur within an abiding context of openness to the Holy Spirit, the animator of grace, truth, and hope in our midst. Don't just start meetings with prayer. Have a prayer campaign that asks parishioners to pray for the abundant coming of the Holy Spirit in order to guide your planning and deliberations. Begin prayer by acknowledging that the Holy Spirit is right here among us; then all we have to pray for is to be open to the Spirit's many gifts such as wisdom, patience, knowledge, courage, and so forth. God's guidance is already among us because the Holy Spirit dwells with us and prepares us for our holy work.

The Rhythm of a Parish Calendar

When should a catechetical leader begin planning for next year? First, when does your parish's year begin? I have found that most parishes begin their fiscal year on July 1. If this is the case, you probably need to have a budget proposal ready to submit by as early as January. I know that many of you may not have much say in the development of your budget or may not even have a budget. Consider discussing this with your pastor or business manager. Don't be afraid to advocate for what you need to strengthen and develop the ministries for which you were hired.

The academic year starts roughly on September 1. Many, if not most, faith-formation ministries in a parish consider this their start time too, when families have returned from summer vacations and as the parish prepares for Catechetical Sunday. Planning for significant paradigm shifts in a religious-education program, for example, should be under way a year or more in advance. Do not, for example, try to change from a classroom school model to a family-formation model in eight months or less.

Even a change of moderate proportion, such as changing the days on which religious education is held, should be prepared for months in advance of implementation. As eager as you and others may be to make positive changes in faith-formation ministries, err on the side of having more than enough time to work a process of discernment and implementation. Change always is messier and takes more time than we expect. It's important to plan well and implement change effectively rather than quickly. One successful change implementation will garner confidence in your leadership for further change.

Different faith-formation ministries have different rhythms to their year. Young-adult and youth ministries often have a relatively active summer pattern, whereas child faith-formation programs tend to be least active in the summer (except for Vacation Bible School). Adult faith-formation ministry is less subject to the academic year and thus ideally can flow in harmony with the liturgical calendar. Catechumenal ministry also can be year round and should follow the flow of the liturgical calendar.

A practical tip is to work within the system of calendaring used at your parish. Get sessions, events, and meetings on the master calendar as early as possible. Leaders of children's ministry will want to coordinate scheduling with the Catholic school, if one is present in the parish. You can also work to obtain calendar information from local public school districts prior to planning the schedule.

Catechetical writer and consultant Joe Paprocki has produced a very practical resource for helping directors and coordinators keep track of the rhythm of a children's religious-education program. Borrowing from Gail Thomas McKenna's *Through the Year with the DRE: A Seasonal Guide for Christian Educators* (now out of print), Joe lists a month-by-month schedule of the typical responsibilities that face directors and coordinators of religious education. You can access this great resource on Joe's blog, www.catechistsjourney.com, by entering the search words "through the year with the DRE." Remember, however, that every parish is different and there are no cookie-cutter faith-formation programs.

Summary: The Lord Directs the Steps

The human mind plans the way,
but the LORD directs the steps. (Prov. 16:9)

Planning is a responsibility of good leadership. But we mustn't fall into the trap of thinking that good planning equals "what I want to happen." Rather, it requires that we involve others and listen well, especially to the Holy Spirit. In a dynamic world of change, we can set goals and be strategic. But our plans must also be flexible.

For Reflection and Discussion

- Do you fear change? What change, and why?
- Parishes can be change resistant and risk averse. How can you help your parish create a culture of openness to a horizon of possibilities and growth?

• Have you been a student of your parish's culture? Do you feel you have your finger on its pulse—its true needs and its potential?

Growing as a Catechetical Leader

Read Fr. James Mallon's excellent book *Divine Renovation*, which inspires and accompanies leaders in their planning for pastoral renewal. Consider how to apply its wisdom (and that of the subsequent *Divine Renovation Guidebook*) to your ministry and to the broader life of the parish.

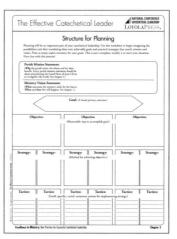

Go to www.loyolapress.com/ECL to access the worksheet.

Suggested Action

Schedule an informal "retreat day" for your staff and/or advisory board (in a relaxed setting off campus, with plenty of good coffee and food). Begin to imagine together how the kingdom of God can be manifested in your parish, and discern a couple of simple goals for how to get there.

For Further Consideration

Divine Renovation: Bringing Your Parish from Maintenance to Mission. James Mallon (New London, CT: Twenty-Third Publications, 2014).

Divine Renovation Guidebook: A Step-by-Step Manual for Transforming Your Parish. James Mallon (New London, CT: Twenty-Third Publications, 2016).

Fostering Leadership Skills in Ministry: A Parish Handbook. Jean Marie Hiesberger (Liguori, MO: Liguori Publications, 2008).

Growing an Engaged Church. Albert L. Winseman (The Gallup Organization, 2006).

Leading Change. John P. Cotter (Boston: *Harvard Business Review,* 2012).

A Practical Guide to Needs Assessment. 3rd ed. Catherine M. Sleezer, Darlene F. Russ-Eft, Kavita Gupta (Pfeiffer Publishing, 2014).

3

Fitting within Church Structures

Entering an Established Culture

Fitting in is not always easy. Think about times you entered into the unfamiliar. What was it like to start at a new school? Or move into a new neighborhood? While it is true that where two or more are gathered, God is present, it is also true that where two or more are gathered, there is an established culture . . . and the politics that goes with it. It is incumbent upon us as the new entity in the mix to learn the rules of engagement and abide by them, at least initially. I say this even if the rules of engagement are dysfunctional and the culture is less than ideal, because there is little chance a new person is going to enter into any social structure and immediately change it.

Too much is at stake for those who are accustomed to the existing structure, and the resistance to change may be great. This doesn't mean that new members of a parish staff should suddenly lose their convictions and their voice. But be smart, prudent, and humble, especially at the start.

My Own Learning Curve

When I started as a twenty-eight-year-old on the staff of a very large suburban parish, I didn't have the wisdom I do now. I did strive to recognize the experience and expertise of my new colleagues and often deferred to them. I was reassured that I was a full partner at the staff table and that I should dive into the deliberations, but I made the mistake of really believing that.

Staff meetings proceeded relatively smoothly, and I was invited to speak my mind and offer ideas for new ways to operate as a parish. However, I soon learned that there were entrenched personalities, an unspoken pecking order, and even feuds and alliances. My what-you-see-is-what-you-get style did not serve me well, and I found myself getting shot down again . . . and again . . . and again. It took me a good year to figure out that I needed to back off, keep learning the culture of the place, and earn my stripes over time. I wish someone had just told me this at the beginning.

Looking back, I have no complaint or resentment. I was actually extremely blessed in my years on that staff, and I learned so much along the way. But it is good for any new catechetical leader, or one coming into a new parish setting, to appreciate that there is always a subtext, a dynamic beneath the surface. Nothing is quite as it might seem. While this might seem unfortunate, it is true. Parishes are not places to go to escape the human condition.

Entering with Humility and Wisdom

Every parish is different. Your current parish is different from the one you may have worked in previously or the one you grew up in. It is different from the neighboring parish and the one next to that. It is vitally important that all parish leaders enter into the culture (and cultures) of a parish with sensitivity and respect. The danger for a veteran catechetical leader coming in new to a parish is to try to impose an approach that worked in a previous parish. The danger for brand-new catechetical leaders is to fail to perceive that a culture exists, or to simply project their image of a parish onto the faith community they have been called to lead and serve. Any such approach lacks the Christian virtue of humility or wisdom, or both.

Whether experienced in catechetical leadership or not, one who is new to a parish should be in "listen and learn" mode as much as possible. There should never be a conversation that does not potentially enrich your understanding of the parish community you have entered. It's amazing how much you can learn by spending time with people and listening . . . and asking good questions. You'll want to become proficient in reading the "subtext" that lies beneath the what-you-see-is-what-you-get surface. And of course, remember that not every perspective you hear will prove to be worthy of consideration. Unfortunately, some folks may attempt to win you over to their narrow cause or their self-serving agenda. So, try to learn how to distill information and discern whom you can trust. This is an important skill for life and for ministry, too.

As you grow in your experience and understanding of your parish, develop deepening collegial relationships with all members of the parish staff, and especially other catechetical leaders on staff. See them as primary cohorts. Also, strive to develop respectful and friendly relationships with administrative and maintenance staff. Your fellow parish staffers can be an invaluable source of information and insight and can help you understand the history of the parish and the interpersonal dynamics in play. They can also help you with the nuts-and-bolts logistical dynamics of a parish, such as how to lock up, where to find coffee filters, and how to schedule for room setup.

The hope is that a leader who is new to a parish will be a conscientious student and a quick study. The learning curve for all of us is never-ending, but it is really steep in the first couple of years. By the third year, you should have a relatively good handle on the cultural dynamics of a parish.

You and Your Pastor

Your pastor, of course, is a primary figure in your development into an effective parish catechetical leader. All of us must remember that the pastor is the chief catechetical leader of a parish. For that reason alone, we must see ourselves as his agent and take his vision and inclinations to heart. Ultimately the pastor is responsible for hiring us and retaining us. Particularly if the pastor hires you, he is invested in you. Your success will reflect well upon him.

Fortunately, the pastor who hired me to be director of parish faith formation was, from the outset, available and helpful. He freely shared his vision for the parish and his inclinations for our faith-formation ministries. He was kind enough to mentor me into the life of the parish. I was smart enough to know that he was ultimately in charge, but I felt empowered by him to use my talents and charisms in forging a leadership style and a direction for the ministries under my care.

Regardless of whether your pastor is a hands-off delegator who doesn't seem much interested in your work, a micromanager who expects you to implement his agenda with precision, or someone who represents a happy medium between those two extremes, you should care what he thinks. Be sure to spend time with him, whether formally or informally. Attempt to draw out his catechetical vision, within the larger context of his pastoral vision for the parish. Hopefully, this can be a dialogic process, with you contributing to a shared vision for the future of faith-formation ministry in the parish.

Canon Law: A Helpful Universal Framework for Ministry

Some of us may hear the term *canon law* and be intimidated. This is understandable. We may believe that canon law is in opposition to being "pastoral" in ministry. This would be incorrect. The purpose of canon law is to regulate the functions of the Church and to protect the rights of the people of God. Canon law is actually very pastoral and not as rigid as one might think.

As parish leaders, we need to be familiar with sections in book 3 of *The Code of Canon Law, The Teaching Office of the Church,* that relate to catechetical instruction (particularly Canons 773–780) and book 4, *The Sanctifying Office of the Church* (particularly the relevant canons on the sacraments). Having a command of these sections of canon law will help you to understand the guidelines of the Universal Church. And on occasion, canon law will prove to be a welcome support for the policies established in the parish, especially those relating to sacramental issues, so long as parish policy is in accord with it.

There is most likely a *Code of Canon Law* book that you can access in the parish. You'll find helpful commentary with each canon to explain its meaning and purpose. Likewise, many dioceses offer workshops and resources on canon law as it pertains to various ministries in the parish, so be sure to contact your diocesan catechetical office.

Shifting from Inside the Parish to Beyond the Parish

Now that we have covered the key relationships that you need to cultivate within the parish, let's turn our attention to key relationships *beyond the parish*:

- *Neighboring parish catechetical leaders* are important people you should get to know and build relationships with. If you are a new leader (or even just new to the area), your colleagues in nearby parishes may be able to provide both personal support and professional mentorship to you. I found having this kind of relationship with a long-time Director of Religious Education (DRE) just down the road to be invaluable as I was beginning in my role. It was great being able to pick up the phone or visit when needed. Find one or more good parish catechetical leaders to help with your mentorship.

Additionally, parishes are increasingly discovering ways to develop shared or joint ministry efforts. (Technology, including quickly-expanding cloud technology, is making it easier for leaders to remotely work on projects together.) Two (or more) parishes can have all the benefits of an offering at a reduced cost to each. In fact, with the sharing of costs, the quality of the offering and the experience for attendees may both be strengthened. I think of three parishes that annually join together for their high-quality catechist-formation series. They wouldn't be able to do it alone. Look to have these kinds of conversations with your nearby colleagues.

- *Deanery/cluster groups (or DRE associations)* can be a powerful source for networking and for personal support and encouragement. As a diocesan director, I see our director/coordinator of religious education (DRE-CRE) deanery groups as one of the most critical indicators of health on our diocesan catechetical landscape. When nurtured properly, these groups form strong bonds and raise the level of faith-formation ministry being delivered in their respective parishes. Here are benefits I see coming from participating in a well-functioning deanery (or cluster) group.

  ◦ The group prays well together . . . and for one another.

  ◦ Effective practices are readily shared, and members come away with good, practical ways to strengthen their ministry and deal with common issues.

  ◦ Shared humor and fun can defuse some of the frustration and anxiety that often enter our ministry and provide a joyful infusion into the calendar.

○ Professional networking leads to the forming of some good friendships.

○ Mutual accountability develops and creates a culture of excellence that makes us all better.

○ Ongoing group formation (theological, spiritual, pedagogical) enriches the ministry leader.

If you don't seem to have a viable deanery or cluster in place, I urge you to explore getting this started. Talk with your diocesan catechetical leader about it. The shared blessings experienced in the deanery groups I've accompanied have been tremendous. Parish catechetical leaders need to be relators and networkers, not just to those above and below them. Our ministry can be demanding and even lonely at times. Having peers to laugh and cry with—and with whom to exchange the fruits of personal giftedness—is more important than you might think.

A practice that has richly blessed catechetical leaders in my diocese is taking turns, at deanery meetings, sharing one's journey of life and faith. This has taken relationships to a deeper level and built a stronger community. This practice is also modeling what we can and should be developing with catechists and with students. Being able to contextualize and articulate one's own faith experience should be a core skill for Catholics—for our own sake and in our efforts to evangelize others. If leaders aren't comfortable and skilled in this, how can we form and train others to do it?

• *Diocesan catechetical directors and staff* are agents of a bishop, who is the chief catechetical leader in a diocese. It is vital that a parish catechetical leader have a relationship with the diocesan catechetical office and, thus, gain the vision for faith formation laid out by one's bishop. In a healthy parish-diocesan partnership dynamic, parish catechetical leaders can feel comfortable and safe in sharing all aspects of their ministry, including difficulties and failings. The primary role for a diocesan catechetical office is to be a resource for helping leaders to grow in ministry effectiveness, while also advocating on behalf of the bishop who is the chief catechist of the diocese.

If your diocesan director or staff person hasn't reached out to you for the purpose of establishing a connection, you can make the first move. Ask him or her to come visit you, and/or set up a time to go and visit the diocesan office. I can assure you that one of the best parts of my role as diocesan catechetical director is getting to visit face-to-face with the parish folks I'm privileged to lead and serve. Phone calls also brighten my day, even when the topic might be challenging.

Don't be shy about building that relationship and utilizing the resources of your diocese (catechetical and other offices). Attend diocesan leadership-formation offerings and participate in its forums. And don't be afraid to offer input to your diocesan director about how the diocese office can better serve your needs.

- *The National Conference for Catechetical Leadership (NCCL)* is the national association designed to promote the agenda of the ministries of catechesis and evangelization in the United States. The NCCL, which started as an organization for diocesan directors and opened membership to parish catechetical leaders in the 1990s, is dedicated to serving the needs of all catechetical leaders through its annual conference and digital resources. Members are invited to participate in the mission and work of the organization.

As a longtime member of the NCCL, I can attest to the organization's commitment to maintaining a high level of faith-formation ministry standards. It is helping diocesan and parish leaders explore how to transmit our Catholic faith with fidelity and effectiveness in each generation. For a modest annual membership fee, you can receive substantial benefit to your ministry, including a national network of catechetical professionals, and also help to support this important national voice of advocacy for our ministry. For information, go to https://www.nccl.org.

- *Catechetical publishing representatives* can be very helpful partners to your ministry. They develop and make resources available to improve the effectiveness of your catechetical program. I have found many members of the publishing community to be truly interested in the welfare of parish faith formation, and they can be a source of information and support. Get to know your publisher representatives and consultants and see how they can be of service to you.

- *The catechetical (and evangelization) offices of the United States Conference of Catholic Bishops (USCCB)* primarily serve bishops and their diocesan staffs. But the USCCB is producing useful, hands-on (and often free) catechetical resources for parishes to utilize. Check out their Web site to learn more: http://www.usccb.org.

Building Relationships

The old adage in the real-estate business says there are three priorities: location, location, location! When it comes to effective catechetical leadership, the priorities are relationships, relationships, relationships! Whether or not you are new to a parish or to the ministry, take time to recognize the overt structures and the underlying cultural dynamics within the community. Build relationships on the solid terrain of integrity and mutuality, and over time, you will be perceived as a trusted colleague and leader in the parish and beyond.

Addendum for Parishes with Catholic Schools

Both a parish faith-formation ministry and a parish Catholic school have the same religious mission: to be centers of evangelization for the children and families they serve. If you serve in a parish with a school, make it a priority to develop close, collegial relationships with school leadership and faculty. In some cases, a parish hires a new catechetical leader with the explicit charge of overseeing faith formation in both the faith-formation program and the school. This sound approach allows for continuity between the two. It says, "We are one parish, with one vision for the formation of children and their families across the spectrum of the community."

If there is a lack of clarity on what is expected in your relationship with the school, have a conversation with your pastor. Learn what his vision is, and then advocate for the building of bridges so that the "one parish" message is communicated. In parishes where the school and the catechetical program have run on separate tracks (parallel or not), it may initially be very difficult to create bridges. In such cases, the pastor may need to provide determined leadership to help reshape the cultural landscape within the parish. Book 6 of this series will further explore the relationship between the catechetical leader and the Catholic school community.

Summary: Two by Two

He called the twelve and began to send them out two by two. (Mark 6:7)

Whether we serve in a large parish or a small one, we contribute to something big and beautiful—the ancient and universal Catholic Church! We are accountable to more than just ourselves. We need to nurture relationships with key stakeholders within the parish—especially with the chief catechetical leader in a parish, the pastor. Beyond the parish, there are structures and people who will support you and help you grow in your leadership role. Stay open to the possibility of growth, not only in knowledge and skills but also in self-awareness.

For Reflection and Discussion

- A parish with a staff that relates well with and trusts one another can do amazing things together. What do you do to foster a sense of team on staff and among key leaders?

- Keep in mind that there are three sides to every story—with the third side being the truth. Do you listen well and gather sufficient information before making judgments? How can you grow in these skills?

- Outside of the parish, whom do you see as potentially supporting you and enriching your catechetical leadership?

Growing as a Catechetical Leader

The *General Directory for Catechesis* reminds us that "catechesis is an essentially ecclesial act" (#78). This suggests that we must never conduct our ministry as a "lone ranger," as one who functions in isolation. There are catechetical leaders around you with gifts and experience that can bless your ministry. Try to get to know them, and be sure to participate in regional or deanery gatherings, always seeking to remind yourself that the ministry you participate in belongs to the whole Church.

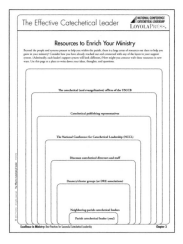

Go to www.loyolapress.com/ECL to access the worksheet.

Suggested Action

Make a list of the people in your life who are honest with you. Do some of them relate to you through your catechetical ministry? Work to create a safe network of people who can give you useful, if sometimes challenging, feedback to help you grow.

For Further Consideration

Emerging Models of Parish Leadership series (Chicago: Loyola Press).

The Pastoral Companion: A Canon Law Handbook for Catholic Ministry. 4th updated ed. John M. Huels (Montreal, Canada: Wilson & Lafleur, 2009).

Principled Ministry: A Guidebook for Catholic Church Leaders. Carroll Juliano and Loughlin Sofield (Notre Dame: Ave Maria Press, 2010).

Who Moved My Cheese? Spencer Johnson, M.D. (New York: G. P. Putnam's Sons, 1998).

4

Catechetical Resources and Models

How Times Have Changed

It is obvious to anyone with eyes to see and ears to hear that our world is rapidly changing. Consider some examples of changes the current generation has brought to everyday living.

- With playlists, we can create our own "radio station."
- With fantasy leagues, we can assemble and "own" our own sports team.
- With our phones, we can create movies/videos without professional help.
- Instead of going to the library to research a topic, we can google it.
- With online matching services, we can select a person to date and *then* meet him or her in person.
- Instead of flying long distances for a family reunion, we can use Skype or FaceTime.

These are just a few examples of how we live differently than we did just a generation ago. Those of us in the digital-immigrant category are challenged to adapt to new ways of doing things. The world and even the hardwiring of the brains of digital natives is changing. Much of what we used to "know" needs to be unlearned, or at least reexamined.

A Shift in Worldview

The cultural chasm that catechetical leaders must grapple with is not limited to the technological realm. There is an equally important (and much thornier) shift of worldview that significantly impacts how we do faith formation. Our world has been steadily and rapidly moving away from a "classical" worldview to what we can call a postmodern—and for some, a post-Christian—worldview. Let's look at the differences between the two views.

- While the classical worldview recognizes a common historical (meta) narrative that informs identity, the postmodern worldview embraces a personal narrative approach while questioning the validity of any overarching meta narrative.

- While the classical worldview implicitly accepts the legitimacy of long-standing institutions, the postmodern worldview inherently mistrusts institutions (including the Church).

- While the classical worldview recognizes an objective truth that applies universally, the postmodern worldview sees the starting point for truth as relative and subjective: what is true for me may not be true for you.

- While the classical worldview insists that the individual conform to accepted norms and practices, the postmodern worldview insists that individuals customize their reality to suit their tastes.

For the catechetical leader, the challenge is to determine how we can effectively transmit Catholic faith and inculcate people—particularly young people—with an understanding of Catholic *community* in a postmodern cultural context. It would seem that the Catholic worldview and the postmodern worldview are inherently at odds with one another. However, along with challenge there is also opportunity for bringing the Catholic faith and the gospel of Jesus into dialogue with a postmodern world.

Engaging with people on their terms in order to begin the conversation that will lead to Jesus is by no means some newfangled approach. *Gaudium et Spes* (*Pastoral Constitution on the Church in the Modern World*) calls for this very approach, and canon law speaks directly to it in Canon #769: "Christian doctrine is to be set forth in a way accommodated to the condition of the listeners and in a manner adapted to the needs of the times." And, of course, it is how Jesus connected with and taught people.

How do we go about religiously engaging a technologically advanced, pluralistic, distracted, and increasingly disbelieving people? This is the seminal question for catechetical leadership today. It should echo in our minds and impact our judgments about how to structure our ministries and programs. It should inform what models we choose and how we use resources.

Jesus as Our Master Catechist

Any consideration of methodology for evangelization and catechesis in our (and any) time should begin with Jesus, the Word Incarnate, who came to embody and convey divine truth and mercy. How did Jesus go about inviting conversion in others? Consider his way of engaging and teaching.

- He met people where they were—in their villages, in their homes, etc.
- He artfully blended pastoral sensitivity with authoritative boldness.
- He used parable storytelling to gain and hold people's attention.
- He often engaged in a dialogue with others and frequently posed questions to draw them out.

- He spoke in a language his audience could understand, using farming and other relatable story lines.

As we move forward to meet the challenges of proclaiming the Good News of Jesus in our rapidly changing world, it is imperative that we avoid simply trotting out resources and methodologies that may have made sense and been effective in the past. This is not the path forward that the Holy Spirit and the Church are calling us to. Jesus himself said, "Neither is new wine put into old wineskins; otherwise, the skins burst, and the wine is spilled, and the skins are destroyed; but new wine is put into fresh wineskins, and so both are preserved" (Matt. 9:17).

The gospel of Jesus Christ is Good News for this and every generation. Jesus' message is one of hope, mercy, healing, and new life for all who surrender to the will of the Father and embrace discipleship to Jesus. The Word of God is eternally new wine. It can never grow stale. So the question becomes, "What will be our containers and delivery systems for God's word?"

Resources for Catechesis and Evangelization

The landscape for resources to be used for Catholic evangelization and faith formation is vast, changing, and growing by the day. It would be impossible to provide a specific and exhaustive listing of good resources here. Further, any fixed list would quickly become dated. More important than trying to give you a fish is helping you know how to fish on your own.

Look for clearinghouse Web sites (one-stop-shopping sites for information and resources) that, in an ongoing manner, revise and update their recommended listing of resources for use in evangelization and catechetical ministry. Of course, any Web site is overseen by people and organizations, with varying degrees of expertise and points of view. Ideally, such clearinghouse Web sites will seek to serve the broad mission of the Church without significant biases or ideological agendas. The National Conference for Catechetical Leadership (www.nccl.org) has been involved with and supportive of two such Web sites, one serving family and parent formation, and one serving Catholic evangelization and evangelizing catechesis. The United States Conference of Catholic Bishops (www.usccb.org) is another reliable source to consult.

As for the use of resources, a few things have become clear as we serve in the current day and look to the future.

- Video has rapidly rivaled the written word as a primary means by which people take in information.

- Digital transmission of information will only increase as the preferred method over paper.

- People's ability and inclination to stay engaged with a particular resource and in a particular mode has, in general, shrunk to a point at which passive learning (such as watching a video) should be limited to a few minutes at a time.

- Mobile devices offer a tremendous opportunity to reach people with formational content wherever they are.

In many ways, we are living in a "golden era" of Catholic faith resources. The strides that have been made to make evangelization and catechetical content engaging and relevant are truly remarkable. This is one of the most exciting developments in the life of the Church in this generation. No doubt the commitment to this will only continue and expand. What is important is that you, along with your staff colleagues and in consultation with your diocesan catechetical office, have the theological acumen to identify those resources that are not only the most engaging but also faithful to Catholic teaching. For example, take care not to assume that just because a video is professionally produced and attractive, you should use it. Properly vet the content.

What we provide must be faithful to Church teaching and should be *Catholic*, not merely a narrow wedge of Catholicism. Remember that you, as catechetical leader, are charged with forming people in the *fullness* of faith, unbiased by any particular ideologies.

Likewise, when considering catechetical resources and models for faith formation, keep in mind the rates by which people tend to retain information and learn, depending on the learning mode. The following graphic demonstrates.

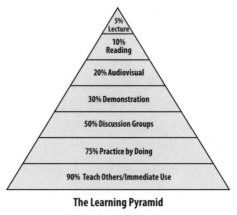

The Learning Pyramid

Finally, both evangelization and catechesis must contextualize faith in relationship to life and the world in which people live. Entirely secular articles and video clips can be used by the artful catechist as fodder for great reflection and discussion. The twentieth-century Swiss Reformed theologian Karl Barth was right in saying, "Take your Bible and take your newspaper, and read both. But interpret newspapers from your Bible." This is at the heart of our ministry: making sense of life in the light of faith. One of the best examples of this methodology today is the practice of Bishop Robert Barron, who brilliantly tackles the issues of the day through the prism of the Catholic worldview.

With all that as a backdrop and a foundation, let's explore a number of catechetical models that are available to you.

Catechetical Models

- *The Rite of Christian Initiation of Adults (RCIA)*—Both the *General Directory for Catechesis* and the *National Directory for Catechesis* call us to view the RCIA as the starting point when exploring models for faith formation. "The baptismal catechumenate is a vital component in the organization of catechesis in the parish. The catechumenate is an essential process in the parish, one that serves as the inspiration for all catechesis" (*NDC*, #54B1). Post-baptismal models for catechesis don't necessarily have to closely imitate the catechumenal model, but all models should look to the catechumenate for values and guiding principles such as "comprehensiveness and integrity of formation; its gradual character expressed in definite stages; its connection with meaningful rites, symbols, biblical and liturgical signs; its constant references to the Christian community" (*GDC*, #91). The RCIA should be the measuring stick for our current catechetical programs to see if they contain essential Catholic qualities for faith development. Whether or not you personally facilitate the RCIA process in your parish, it is imperative that you know, understand, and appreciate the character of the process of initiation in order to pattern your other catechetical efforts after it.

- *RCIA Adapted for Children*—This is the proper title for what some call the "RCIC" ("Rite of Christian Initiation for Children") or "Children's Catechumenate." It is, as the name suggests, a process of initiating children and youth into the Catholic faith in close adherence to the principles and directives of the Rite of Christian Initiation of Adults (RCIA), which allows for and encourages adaptation of the rites to honor the particular needs of children and youth (#253). This process should meet children where they are developmentally, both in age and in faith experience. It is *essential* to engage parents in the process, seeking to foster conversion in them, too (see chapter 9). Normatively, children in this process are fully initiated at the Easter Vigil, although exceptions can be made as to the timing. Catechumens, or the unbaptized, are to receive all three sacraments of initiation together. Candidates, or baptized children, are to complete their initiation with reception of the Eucharist and confirmation.

• *Children "Out of Sequence"*—Increasingly, the Church in the United States has been experiencing an increase in the number of families presenting children to parish faith-formation programs who are not baptized or who have not received First Communion at a normative age. It seems likely that this phenomenon will continue to grow. Parish catechetical leaders experience this as both an opportunity and a challenge to connect with and mentor a young person (and his or her family) into Catholic faith and life. However, adapting structures and ministries to meet the needs of diverse families who are not "normative" can be complicated and highly labor intensive. To understand the background of a particular family and judge how best to serve their faith-development needs, it is most important to take time to get to know the family. Pastoral listening will not only build essential trust in your relationship with them but also will help you to assess how to proceed in their pastoral and catechetical care. In some cases, particularly when there has been some degree of connection with the Catholic faith, it might be appropriate and sufficient to place the children in a track that focuses on "religion readiness" so that they can more easily join their peers in the faith-formation program. In other cases, where there has been a real absence of faith life and practice, participation by the child and his or her family in the catechumenal process or a process that parallels the catechumenate will be more appropriate.

- *Parish-Based Child Schooling (Traditional) Model*—Typically, this model occurs on the parish grounds, be it in a parish school or other available and appropriate space. Some parishes locate their faith-formation sessions off-site, either at a nearby school or facility or in parishioners' homes. (The latter presents child-safety issues that must be addressed, insofar as the setting is less "controlled.") The schooling model, characterized by grade-level classes with grade-level textbooks and catechists, is considered by many the *traditional* mode for transmission of the faith. However, this model is a less organic and more recent approach than that which has occurred through every century in Christian homes. The schooling model, when done effectively, has advantages that should be appreciated.

  ◦ The parish has strong oversight of the catechetical content and process.

  ◦ Catechists are vetted, prepared, supported, and evaluated to ensure quality control.

  ◦ Children are exposed, in most cases, to the parish facilities, personnel, and culture.

  ◦ Children are socialized in a Catholic setting with their peers.

  However, even in parishes in which the schooling model is done magnificently, challenges remain. The rate of active practice of the Catholic faith among youth and young adults today is distressingly low and dropping still further. This model, likewise, suffers from what can be called the "drop-off" mentality, which can encourage parents to assume that faith formation is primarily the responsibility of the parish religious-education program and its catechists. This kind of mentality prompted Pope Francis to call upon parents to "return from their exile" to assume their proper role in the formation of their children.

In truth, many catechetical leaders and pastoral ministers have long recognized that a strict reliance on the schooling model for passing on the Catholic faith is insufficient. It perpetuates an approach that served well in bygone days when faith was supported and nurtured robustly by the family, the community, and the culture as a whole. Today, those support systems have either deteriorated or completely collapsed, leaving faith formation an isolated activity that accounts for approximately 3/1000ths of a young person's year! This reality is leading us to explore new paradigms for faith formation, many of which rightly place an emphasis on the role of the family and on parents as the primary educators of their children. In order to maximize the benefits of the schooling model, the following actions are imperative:

- Give emphasis and priority to catechist formation. The schooling model places great responsibility on the role of the catechist, which means that your primary responsibility as the catechetical leader is to ensure that catechists are properly formed and eminently capable of assuming that role.
- Look to utilize the full resources of the parish to flesh out and integrate the presentation of the Catholic faith. We are not catechizing children to ultimately pass a Confirmation test. We are initiating young people into an active Catholic life within the parish context and the out-in-the-world context.
- Continually engage parents (or guardians) in the faith-formation experience of their children. At every turn find ways to communicate with parents, build relationships, and strive to invite them into their own journey on the path of evangelization and catechesis.

The schooling model will no doubt continue to have a place in the future of Catholic faith formation. However, for it to be effective, it must be an element in an approach that is designed with organic integration into the home, the broader life of the parish, and, indeed, the world! An isolated, stand-alone schooling model that focuses largely on the transmission of information will continue to fail to provide us with young people who know God personally and love and live their Catholic faith passionately.

• *Intergenerational (Whole Parish) Model*—As we mentioned earlier, catechetical leaders are becoming increasingly aware of the inadequacy of the traditional schooling model and its "drop-off" mentality. Fortunately, pioneering catechetical leader John Roberto led a widespread campaign in the early 2000s to broaden parish faith-formation efforts beyond just children to all Catholics of all ages. He helped parish leaders in dioceses across the country understand that the schooling model was successful only because of the context in which it took place in prior decades. The intergenerational approach invites families and people of all ages to gather regularly as a community for formational experiences tied to themes of the Catholic faith and the liturgical year. Intergenerational experiences usually include segments for the whole group together combined with shorter segments for specific age groups. The strengths of this approach are the building of a sense of community, the opportunity for families to experience faith formation together, and an emphasis on faith formation as being lifelong, which is an essential insight. (As I'm often saying, our graduation from faith development is not Confirmation but, rather, death.) Logistical challenges come with this large-group approach to faith formation, and facility limitations are a part of this.

We now stand at a place in history when a lifelong and intergenerational approach to Catholic formation makes more sense than ever. In terms of practical reality, we have far too many adults who are in need of an *evangelizing catechesis* designed to invite conversion and draw them into the richness of Catholic belief and practice. And without bringing a "new evangelization" or a "re-evangelization" (as called for by Saint John Paul II in *Redemptoris Missio*) to our parents, our Catholic parish programs and schools will continue to sacramentalize their children and send them out into a world that will, in too many cases, overwhelm their Catholic faith. Whole-parish faith formation has the right instinct for what is needed today in the Church. We need to embrace a vision in which all parishioners are candidates for ongoing formation and conversion. It is a goal to imagine, work toward, and achieve as the circumstances of your parish allow.

• *Family Faith-Formation Model*—In *The Joy of Love*, Pope Francis affirms the place of parents in the formation of their children: "[C]ouples and parents should be properly appreciated as active agents in catechesis. . . . Family catechesis is of great assistance as an effective method in training young parents to be aware of their mission as the evangelizers of their own family" (*Amoris Laetitia*, #287). The centrality of parents in the formation of children is explored in greater depth in chapter 9. Here, it should suffice to point out the obvious. If we fail to include parents (grandparents, guardians, and other adults important in the life of children), we are doing both them and their children a grave injustice. Parents grow in their faith through their children, and children grow in faith in relationship to their parents. The family is designed by God to be the place where faith most organically blossoms and develops. Our past (and current) methods that substitute the parish or school for the home are misaligned to both our theology and our nature.

The family faith-formation model is essentially a subset of the intergenerational model and is flexible enough to vary from parish to parish according to needs, culture, and limitations of a parish. Typically, this model gathers families together once per month. There is a session together, and then separately. The children meet with their own age groups while the adults engage in quality adult faith formation including small-group discussions and brief video segments related to the doctrinal theme of the session. The parents are then equipped to work with their children on the successive lessons of that month's unit at home. They can use an at-home edition of an approved catechetical text, online activities provided by the publisher, and other suggestions for engaging in two key activities—*God talk* and *Catholic practices*—as a family. Through online or other modes of assessment that the children complete at the end of each lesson, the catechetical leader is able to monitor progress and reach out to families when needed. Wise parishes also provide a menu of parish experiences and require families to select a certain number to participate in so as to reinforce the bonds between the family and the faith community as a whole.

If you are considering shifting to this model (or any new model), please do not rush into it. Take the time to educate, equip, and prepare parents for embracing their role as their child's primary educator. In addition, parishes often introduce this model as an alternative at first, so as not to abandon people who are not yet ready to make the change.

I've seen various family models make a real difference in the lives of parents and their children in my years serving parishes as a diocesan director. Denise Utter, one parish practitioner of this catechetical model with whom I've served and who is now a national advocate for it, offers, "Encouraging families in this model, empowering them to talk about God and live faith at home and in the community, allows parents to build confidence as the primary faith formators in their family." From my perspective, *how* family faith formation is designed deserves considerable, ongoing attention. *That* family formation should be embraced is no longer even a question. The time has come for its widespread integration into our ministry, be it to a smaller degree or greater degree!

- *Catechesis of the Good Shepherd (CGS)*—This model is a Montessori-style catechesis (through sixth grade) that is heavily grounded in Scripture, liturgy, and moral formation. CGS is a very hands-on approach and attempts to inculcate a reflective spirituality beginning in early childhood. This can be a valuable complement to traditional models. Parishes would be wise to learn from the CGS instincts for faith formation. CGS requires a dedicated space as well as specialized materials and catechist training. This model, developed and championed by the late Sofia Cavelletti along with her colleague Gianna Gobbi, is especially effective with children in early childhood and primary grades through its emphasis on Scripture stories, the liturgical life of the Church, tactile learning, and contemplation.

- *Special Needs Faith Formation*—This teaching model offers helpful adaptations and assistance for children, youth, and adults who have special needs. A catechetical leader should explore the possibility of including these individuals into existing structures with their peers. This may require providing an aide or making other adjustments. However, if a person's special needs are too great to allow for inclusion, separate programming should be made available, ranging from group sessions with others who have similar needs to individual instruction. And particular pastoral care must be extended to these families, communicating the warm embrace and support of the parish community. (This important aspect of catechetical ministry is treated in greater depth in book 6 of this series, *All God's People*.) While every parish may not be able to be fully attentive to the broad range of special needs, attention and planning should be conducted by dioceses and regions so that no family needs to travel a burdensome distance to receive the care and attention they deserve.

- *Sacramental Readiness*—Some people may view as avant garde the increasing use of *readiness* as the standard for conferring sacraments. In actuality, this was the first model in the early Christian church. People received sacraments when they were deemed ready. There is a bold advocacy, led by Fr. James Mallon (pastor and author of *Divine Renovation),* for restoring this approach for children as we do for adults. Given the challenges we outlined at the outset of this chapter, such creative and seemingly risky approaches that focus on the heart of our mission—conversion to Christ Jesus—should be welcomed and further explored. The truth is, the readiness approach is not all that risky. We fear that we will lose people if we move away from the schooling model. But do we really have those folks to begin with?

- *Additional Catechetical Models*—We have devoted our attention here to the more prominent catechetical models, but there are many additional ones. While they can receive only brief mention here, these models carry significant potential value in the formation of both children and adults and warrant further study.

  - **Lectionary-Based Formation**: catechesis that draws on the Scripture readings for the upcoming Sunday
  - **Children's Liturgy of the Word**: a liturgical action in which children are called from the assembly after the Opening Prayer (Collect) of the Mass to go with a catechist to hear and reflect on the Scripture readings before returning at the Offertory
  - **Home-Schooling**: parents assume full responsibility for the faith formation of their child in cooperation with the parish.

- ○ **Summer Intensive:** a two- or three-week catechetical session during the summer that meets four or five days a week for several hours instead of once a week for an hour throughout the year.

Summary: The New and the Old

"Every scribe who has been instructed in the kingdom of heaven is like the head of a household who brings from his storeroom both the new and the old." (Matt. 13:52, NABRE)

Jesus doesn't leave his apostles a user's manual with steps 1-2-3 and mandatory methods a-b-c for running his Church. Instead, he invites us into relationship, he sheds light on the truth, he teaches some principles, he accustoms us to good ministry. Ground yourself in good theology, spirituality, morality, and pedagogy. Study the real people (and their culture) you're trying to reach. And then be a curator or discerning manager of good resources and models that will serve well in your time and place. It seems clear that the resources and models of the future will not resemble a strictly book-and-classroom approach.

For Reflection and Discussion

- We can easily fall into lamenting the loss of the "good ol' days." What good do you see in today's culture? What opportunities does it offer for evangelization and catechesis?
- What models are you currently using in your parish ministries, and why? What outcomes do they produce?

Growing as a Catechetical Leader

Look again at the points describing Jesus as our Master Catechist on page 43. Which of these items speaks to your heart as something you want to better incorporate into your leadership style?

Go to www.loyolapress.com/ECL to access the worksheet.

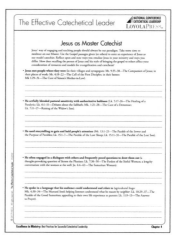

Suggested Action

Discuss the models mentioned in this chapter with your RE advisory board or pastor in light of the parish's catechetical/evangelization vision. Consider in what ways your parish is currently functioning in *maintenance* mode—and how it should shift more into *mission* mode.

For Further Consideration

Children of the Light: Precatechumenate Sessions for Children and Families. Blessie LaScola (World Library Publications, 2016).

Common Sense Catechesis: Lessons from the Past, Road Map for the Future. Fr. Robert J. Hater (Huntington, IN: Our Sunday Visitor, 2014).

Families at the Center of Faith Formation. Leif Kehrwald, John Roberto, Gene Roehlkepartain, Jolene Roehlkepartain (Naugatuck, CT: Lifelong Faith Associates, 2016).

Guide to Adapting the RCIA for Children. Rita Burns Senseman (Liturgy Training Publications, 2017).

National Directory for Catechesis. (Washington, DC: United States Conference of Catholic Bishops, 2005).

The Religious Potential of the Child: 6 to 12 Years Old. Sofie
    Cavalletti (Catechesis of the Good Shepherd Publications,
    2007).

Rite of Christian Initiation of Adults. (Chicago: Liturgy Training
    Publications, 1988).

*To Heal, Proclaim, and Teach: The Essential Guide to Ministry in
    Today's Catholic Church.* Jared Dees (Notre Dame, IN: Ave
    Maria Press, 2016).

The Way of Faith: A Field Guide for the RCIA Process. Nick Wagner
    (New London, CT: Twenty-Third Publications, 2008).

5

Operational Aspects: Out Front and Behind the Scenes

Putting on Your Game Face

Not all moments in ministry are created equal. Some are less public, where tasks are being accomplished without fanfare. And some are very public, where impressions are being made and relationships are being furthered (or harmed).

This wasn't entirely clear to me in my early months as a DRE. I still recall the day, after an evening meeting of the parish council, when I was modestly read the riot act by my pastor for being a sullen bump-on-the-log during the meeting. I had been invited to listen to (and contribute to) a discussion on broad parish visioning. For some reason, I thought it was okay not to bring energy, not to be engaged, not to be particularly personable that evening.

I probably made a lousy impression on members of the parish council that night. And I was wrong on every count mentioned above. Regardless of whether I had a tough day, a long week, was out-of-sorts or whatever, I needed to put on my game face and perform at a high level, with professionalism, energy, and as much charm as I could muster.

High-Impact Ministry Moments

The truth is that some dimensions of catechetical leadership demand a higher degree of energy and emoting than others. Some moments are what I call "high impact"—times that call on us to be at our best, to shine. While administration functions are important and will be addressed later in this chapter, those are not the high-impact opportunities I'm referring to.

High-impact ministry occurs when we are with other people. This happens at staff meetings, parish council meetings, advisory board meetings, parent and family formation events, or any time parishioners are gathered for a ministry offering that you oversee or relate to, whether you are leading it or not. Ministry is primarily relational. Whenever you are with a group of people in your capacity as a catechetical leader, you are engaging, to one degree or another, in high-impact ministry. For the extrovert reading this book, this is good news. For the introvert, this is important news. Just like at Thanksgiving or any holiday when the host cannot hide in a bedroom, a catechetical leader must be a gracious, attentive, and even charming welcomer and moderator of gathered people.

Religious-Education Session: It's Game Time!

Catechist formation gatherings and parent/family sessions are among the highest-impact moments in the life of a parish catechetical leader. The hope is that you have a relatively full tank for engaging with these important groups of people in these key moments of opportunity, or at least enough in the tank to be able to power through and be a joyful, energized, and attractive presence. Let's explore a prime aspect of the catechetical leader's role: being the orchestra leader of the exciting, messy, sometimes crazed, and fun time before, during, and after a parish faith-formation session.

Before the Session

1. Have someone in the faith-formation office available in the pre-session hours to take phone calls concerning questions and reports of absences, both for children and for catechists. These calls will create more tasks—calling substitute catechists (you can never have too many good subs!) and making adjustments for the session.

2. Be on-site early to greet the first of the early-arriving catechists (who should be there before their early-arriving students). Remain visibly present and available as families start to arrive for the session. You are the host, the leader, the tour guide, the consoler, and the friendly face of the parish. Don't underestimate the substance in the symbolism of your pastoral presence.

3. To accomplish the above point and be appropriately available before and throughout the session, sufficient support must be in place prior to the session:

   - someone positioned to take phone calls at the session location
   - an administrative team: people making last-minute copies, taking attendance, managing equipment and resources (better to have extra support than not enough)
   - security presence: hall monitors and, if needed, parking lot attendants

It takes many hands on deck to run a smooth catechetical session. Be sure to invite and attract good people suitable to these roles, and then train and empower them to serve with grace and effectiveness. This is your game-day operations team.

During the Session

1. As program leader, you may want to make any initial announcements over the PA system or at a gathering of all the participants. This is another chance to welcome everyone, set a positive tone, and provide needed information to begin the session.

2. Early into the session, secure the building. After that, a system should be in place to screen anyone wishing to enter the building. Both children and adults will need to check in at the office or desk.

3. One of the session staff personnel (paid or volunteer) should be at the main staging area—a key central location or visible and accessible office—throughout the session. This person oversees operations and is the initial point of contact for managing questions and issues that arise.

4. Attendance taking is vital to know which children are absent. Any unanticipated absences require contacting parents immediately. A team member or two should be available to make these calls without delay. (Parent phone numbers must be available on-site for this reason and in case of illness and serious disciplinary matters.)

5. As leader, be out and about as much as possible during the session. Walk the halls. Observe the goings-on both in the classrooms and in the halls. You should have a game plan for which rooms you will want to visit to observe. Visitations can be planned in advance with the catechist. (Formal evaluation opportunities should be mutually planned.) Informal visits can also be impromptu. And, if you sense problems in rooms, you are free to drop in to assess and see if you can be of support to the catechist.

6. As you drop in on classrooms, jump in to echo what the catechist is saying or to pose a question for the children so that the children can experience you as a catechist and so the catechist can benefit from any good modeling you can provide. (Don't typically disrupt the flow of the lesson for too long.)

7. Check in at the main staging area on occasion to see if there are issues requiring your attention. (Cell calling, texting, or using a walkie-talkie can keep you in the know in real time.) Gauge which issues deserve your attention during valuable session time (a serious disciplinary issue, a very agitated parent, etc.). Delegate other matters to your staff, according to their abilities, so that you can mostly perform leadership functions exclusive to your role.

After the Session

1. Again, be strategically positioned to say a joyful goodbye and thank both catechists and children (and parents). It is a difficult balance dealing with an upset (or friendly) parent or catechist while also trying to connect with everyone. The person may understand that you are busy and will be open to waiting a few minutes to talk in depth. Don't get buttonholed unless there is a truly urgent matter. Turn on any charm you have in this especially high-impact moment. Leave folks with a great impression!

2. Meet with your session staff to debrief any issues you need to know about. If you wish to communicate a concern you have, consider whether it is better to discuss in the present moment or later.

3. You and the staff need to assess each space used to ensure it is restored to proper condition.

4. The entire building and grounds must be checked for any remaining children. You and another session team member must remain with any such children in a safe setting until their parents arrive.

There are many moving parts to a parish faith-formation session! I've named only a few key elements. The most important principle is to be visible, to interact, and to orchestrate during this high-impact time of ministry. A catechetical leader should avoid being holed up in a back room, busy moving furniture, or tied up on the phone. I urge you to try to build up a session staff who can manage the tasks and lesser duties of the session, allowing you to be free to lead. And build up that substitute catechist list, too. *The leader should not be performing as a substitute catechist.* Finally, you will find people coming up to you during sessions, giving you information and asking things of you. It is entirely fair to ask them to kindly e-mail you on the matter so that you will remember it. Don't feel bad about doing this.

Administrating a Faith-Formation Program

While few of us may have entered into catechetical leadership because we enjoy policies and paperwork, administrating is a key dimension of the role. Without healthy administration, there would be chaos. It is helpful to revisit the word *administration*, which literally means "toward ministry." At my interview for my diocesan position back in the day, I remember saying that administration was a "necessary evil." And I remember being appropriately challenged on that perspective by a member of the diocesan religious-education board. While administrative tasks may not have the glamour of the interpersonal ministry moments that I call high-impact, they are necessary and allow good ministry to happen.

Strive to "right-size" the support staffing of your faith-formation office so that you are not so bogged down with administrative tasks that you can't provide leadership. Advocate for what is needed, and create a job description for such a position. Look to hire someone with the skill set for and interest in accomplishing these tasks. However, also look for someone with a complementarity of gifts to balance your gifts and make you more effective. For example, if you are a "piler," be sure to look for a "filer." The goal is to create a team—true in any staffing dynamic—in which the sum is greater than the parts.

Systems Are Your Friend!

Our brains are wired to encourage the formation of habits so that each time we perform a task, the brain will not have to start from scratch but can follow a routine. The more you and your staff create and adhere to good systems in your ministry, the more efficiently you will administrate the programs you oversee. Let's briefly explore some notable dimensions of catechetical administration (with particular focus on child programming).

Record Keeping—There is a lot to record and retain in catechetical ministry, particularly when children are involved. Here are some key areas.

- *Catechist Information*: A hard copy and/or digital file should be maintained for each catechist, including personal information and emergency contact/medical information, safe environment compliance, documentation of noteworthy occurrences, record of formational activity over the years and achievement of levels of certification, evaluation forms, information about formational interests/needs, and plans for future development for ministry. Any records relating to the Charter for the Protection of Minors (criminal background checks, fulfillment of diocesan safe-environment training modules) must be permanently retained (even after a catechist leaves) according to diocesan guidelines.

- *Child Information*: A hard copy and/or digital file is to be created, maintained, and permanently retained for each child, including registration, medical and field-trip permission forms, emergency contact information, progress reports, and documentation of parent communications and noteworthy occurrences. All forms with parent signatures must be retained according to diocesan guidelines.

- *Program Information*: Class rosters and attendance records must be retained according to diocesan guidelines.

- *Incident Documentation*: A detailed record of any incidents involving health, safety, inappropriate conduct (and discipline), property damage, and other significant developments must be retained and may be (securely) digitized. This would include your documentation and that of others involved.

- *Family Financial Account (Tuition) Records*: A file to record financial payment activity is to be kept, typically using a parish software program. Any special arrangements should be noted.

Budgeting—Developing an annual budget should be a part of every parish catechetical program and ministry. Budgeting should be understood as investing more than just spending, and it doesn't have to be as scary a task as it might seem. Budgeting goes hand in hand with planning. (See chapter 2 for a deeper consideration of planning.) The first step in creating a budget is to engage in a timely planning process for the next fiscal (financial) year in ministry. Most parishes start their new fiscal year on July 1, which would suggest that budgeting should be conducted in the winter and concluded by the spring. For elements of your ministry that remain relatively stable from year to year, budgeting can be pretty straightforward. Work out the costs and expected revenues related to the new and continuing ministry activities. Use realistic assumptions in this process. Fight the natural temptation to be overly optimistic. Submit your plan and budget as called for by the pastor (or the parish finance council). It will be returned to you as either approved or needing dialogue and/or revision.

If your parish does not engage in a dialogic budgetary process, discuss the situation with your pastor or business manager. Simply giving you, as a catechetical leader, a set amount of money to spend will not be helpful to anyone. On one side, this arbitrarily limits you and others in any plans for growth and development. On the other side, it may result in spending that is not wise stewardship of parish funds. (This is often called the "use it or lose it" approach to a budget.) Another common approach is for parishes and their ministries to function with no budget at all. This leaves a ministry leader unable to plan with any confidence. Again, discuss and advocate for a better approach to ministry planning and financial administration.

Generating Revenue—There are two sides to every financial ledger and every budget: expenses and revenue. Often, it is the expense side that gets all the attention. Don't forget about revenue. I say this with the hope that revenue generation is not a major focus in your ministry. Ideally, it shouldn't be. But with increasing stresses on parish bottom lines often comes increased pressure for religious-education programs to bring in money to the parish. If fund-raising is required for your program, utilize your advisory board to get a sense of what kinds of activities and events families would enjoy. Try to include a parish community-building dimension to it and not just have it be a money-grab. You might also think about creating a program through which parishioners and parish organizations can "adopt" a child or family to help defray their faith-formation costs. This can be both a way to help fund children from homes with financial constraints and also a way for empty nesters and seniors to connect with young families. Always be on the lookout for win-wins.

Parish leaders should always keep in mind that catechetical ministry is named in canon law as a responsibility of a parish and a right of the people of God. Faith formation is a foundational element to the life of a parish. It does not exist primarily to be a funding source to the parish. Rather, it is one of the areas in which a parish must *invest* for the spiritual welfare of its people. Translation: a parish should subsidize its catechetical operations (from its offertory giving) to a substantial degree.

Tuition—Tuition and fees are typically the large majority of revenue generated in a catechetical program. Here are some thoughts on tuition structure and policy.

- Pay attention to neighboring parish tuition rates. Sometimes, differentials are so great that people will choose to register at an alternative program in order to save money. Try to work with neighboring parishes to create a just and relatively consistent tuition approach that mitigates this.

- Consider the economic demographics and living costs in your area. An appropriate tuition schedule will generate optimal revenue without unduly burdening parishioners or risking their departure from the religious-education program.

- In consultation with the pastor and parish finance council, establish guidelines for managing cases where a family is unable to pay all or any of the set tuition and fees. Never should a family be left without access to parish catechetical resources because of an inability to pay. Nor should they be made to feel lesser members of the community. We must treat such people with the full dignity they deserve. At the same time, parishes are within their rights to encourage some manner of payment plan, to invite a volunteer role in consideration of pay, and even to ask for some evidence of hardship to validate full or partial scholarship. Catechetical leadership means continually balancing caring for families and individuals with serving the greater good (in this case, sound financial stewardship) of the parish community.

When dealing with families over tuition issues, be sure to engage them in what I call the "evangelizing conversation" (do it in person, please). This approach creates an opportunity (do it in person, please) to discuss a tuition situation within the more important context of a family's degree of engagement in the life of the parish. The conversation needs to be almost entirely about Christ and Catholic faith and life . . . not about money. Done with love and care, it will be a constructive ministry moment. And, from my experience, some families will enter more fully into an active Catholic lifestyle. They just need to be personally invited and encouraged!

Registration—While aspects of this topic are also treated in chapter 6, let me offer a few points here. The best time to begin the registration season for the following year is before the final RE session (or even *during* the final session). In this way, you will have some idea of how many catechists, textbooks, and various supplies and resources will be needed. Offer discounts for registering early. This allows time for follow-up through the summer and into the fall. Registration packets should include the following:

- information on tuition schedule (suggest talking to the leader about difficulties paying)
- request for normal and emergency contact information
- medical information form (with all pertinent health information, including allergies, ADHD diagnoses, and a medical action plan for children with serious conditions)
- invitation and form for parent to participate in a volunteer role

Some parishes are moving to online registration, although getting parental signatures (on paper or digitally) remains necessary. Make every effort to register new families in person in order to establish a relationship. There is also a move to online payment processing as well, which can result in greater convenience and more efficient collection.

Finally, if your catechetical office closes for part of the summer, be sure the parish office has information about the program, including on registration and collection of fees. Don't make people wait to register.

Program Handbooks for Parents—The annual program handbook that is made available to parents prior to each catechetical year can be offered in hard copy or digital format. Understand that such a handbook is not only an important summary of information for parents to know but also a legal document that allows for children's participation in the program. Whether digital or on hard copy, getting signatures from parents and/or guardians expressing consent to the contents of the handbook is necessary. Elements that are standard in program handbooks include

- a welcome message, ideally from both the pastor and the catechetical leader (remember, every communication should be intentionally designed to feed into the life of the parish)
- an at-a-glance overview, staff names and contact information (a refrigerator magnet or such is also a good way to keep important program information handy)
- statements of vision and purpose for the program
- a detailed overview and a calendar for the full program (particular program schedules, such as sacramental preparation, can be included here or in separate materials for those families)
- information about catechists (training and requirements)
- policies and procedures, including
  - admission policies (program and sacraments)
  - registration process
  - attendance policies
  - program-family relationship, including expectations/ requirements for parental involvement and a system for communication

- ° traffic plan for drop-off and pick-up
- ° visitor and early-release policies
- ° procedures for extraordinary or emergency occasions (weather, lockdown, fire)
- ° medical (including medication) policies and procedures
- ° progress-report information
- ° discipline and dismissal policies and procedures (a "covenant of conduct" signed by the child, parent/guardian, and catechetical leader is a constructive approach to framing discipline)
- ° various and sundry: attire, electronic devices, snacks, weapons

- faith-formation commission/RE board information
- building and parish campus maps
- pertinent diocesan policies and required resources (including but not limited to protection of minors' information)
- a brief and positive bullet-point summary of the parish-family covenant—what the parish asks of parents and families and what parents and families can expect from the parish—is a great last item on the page requiring their signature

Assessment and Progress Reports—Many philosophies exist regarding how to assess learning and integration in religious-education programs. On one extreme, there is the approach that makes parish formation feel much like school. On the other, no assessment is conducted. Somewhere in the middle lies an appropriate balance whereby learning and integration of the content of the Catholic faith are measured in some manner, and families and catechists are invited to a degree of accountability. (I remember author and speaker Patrick Lencioni saying in a presentation that "accountability is love.") Notice that we need to assess learning *and* integration. Our goal is not simply for children to know what they believe but also for them to live out their Catholic faith. Strive to have this value reflected in your approach to assessment. Progress reports, if offered, should be a general assessment of progress and not simply the assignment of a grade.

Charter for the Protection of Children and Young People—Since 2002, all dioceses in the United States have developed and overseen processes in keeping with the Charter for the Protection of Children and Young People, to ensure that all minors within the care of the Church are safe. Responsibility for the parish administration of required procedures varies from parish to parish. In some cases, a parish catechetical leader is the designated administrator. Elements of this responsibility include

- proper vetting of catechists, including completion of a criminal background check and training about safe-environment policies and procedures
- provision of related safety training and periodic review for minors and parents
  - Parents have the ability to opt their children out from such training if they wish to do it themselves at home.
  - In some cases, comparable training in public schools can be accepted in lieu of parish training.
- management of all required paperwork

Parish administrators must consult their local diocese for specific direction in this important effort. Good communication about this topic will help ensure safe environments for ministry with minors, as well as help position the Church as a powerful force for reducing the occurrence of sexual abuse of minors in our society. What a worthy goal! While elements of this administration can seem onerous at times, stay focused on the larger, vital good of this work.

Special Administrative Issues—Finally, here are various details that must be decided on as part of your operational and administrative systems.

- *Custodial Issues*: Be sure to have legal documentation that indicates the custodial status of each parent. The status will determine what rights and access a parent will have.

- *Emergency Procedures*: Establish a set procedure for emergencies such as fire, tornado, and intruder lockdown. Provide related information to catechists and families. Conduct drills to ensure an orderly and effective response.

- *Attendance Issues*: Some children will have very spotty patterns of attendance. In cases of legitimate illness or family difficulties, parishes need to extend pastoral care and provide flexibility in applying policy. (Remember the caution of Pope Francis: "Frequently we act as arbiters of grace rather than its facilitators. But the Church is not a tollhouse; it is the house of the Father, where there is a place for everyone, with all their problems." (*Evangelii Gaudium*, 47) If children are missing classes due to sports and other activities, you should pastorally engage the family *prior* to a discussion of dismissal or nonmatriculation. Seek a balanced outcome so that the children do not feel punished and the high valuing of faith formation is properly retained. Lean on sound, established, and well-communicated policy as the starting point for a pastoral conversation.

- *Field Trips*: If permitted, catechists and parents must know that they will occur only with explicit approval of the catechetical leader. Any off-site activity triggers the need for a special permission form to be completed by parents. Consult diocesan policy and access approved forms.

- *Textbook Review*: Periodically conduct an evaluation with stakeholders (catechists and families). If a formal review and selection process is needed, enlist the RE board to accompany you in this process. Consult diocesan curriculum policies and the quarterly *Conformity Listing of Catechetical Texts and Series* (from the USCCB) for approved options.

Not every aspect of administration has been addressed here. Consult current parish processes, neighboring parish leaders, and your diocese for further guidance. And keep in mind that even at its most mundane, administration is always in service to ministry that is pastoral and formative. Always strive to see it in this positive, valued context.

Summary: A Lampstand with Purpose!

"No one who lights a lamp hides it away or places it under a bushel basket, but on a lampstand so that those who enter might see the light." (Luke 11:33, NABRE)

Administering your program is providing the lampstand on which ministry can shine. Keep this in mind as you strive to keep records in order, prepare your budget, and deal with the details of registration, parent handbooks, and progress reports. Ministry is highly relational, so make sure you have "enough in the tank" to shine brightly during high-impact moments.

For Reflection and Discussion

- Is faith-formation ministry given adequate administrative staffing in your parish to allow you to lead and develop ministries?

- James W. Frick, a longtime Notre Dame University administrator, said, "Don't tell me where your priorities are. Show me where you spend your money, and I'll tell you what they are." What does your current budget say about faith-formation priorities? How should it change to reflect your vision and that of the parish?

- Name an area of administration that you most dislike. By developing a *systematic* approach to it, you can tame the chaos and make it less of an enemy.

Growing as a Catechetical Leader

Author Ann Garrido explains in her book *Redeeming Administration*, "[I]f we are attentive to the potential grace present in the day-to-day responsibilities we tackle as administrators, we can be formed and molded in profound ways. The key is to be aware of and open to the invitation each day" (9). Develop the practice of taking time to name the grace present in your day, including in the small stuff . . . and sometimes even in the hard stuff.

Go to www.loyolapress.com/ECL to access the worksheet.

Suggested Action

When you feel overwhelmed or unable to creatively problem-solve, step away for a walk or prayer or a conversation with a friend. Hitting the reset button might also mean returning to something after a day or two.

For Further Consideration

> *The Effective DRE: A Skills Development Series: Keeping Records and Budgets.* Ruth Bradley and Mary Ann Taeger (Chicago: Loyola Press, 1998).

Everything about Parish Ministry I Wish I Had Known. Kathy Hendricks (New London, CT: Twenty-Third Publications, 2012).

Redeeming Administration. Ann M. Garrido (Notre Dame, IN: Ave Maria Press, 2013).

Religious Education, Parish and Youth Ministry: Legal Issues for Catechetical and Youth Leaders. Mary Angela Shaughnessy, SCN (Washington, DC: National Catholic Educational Association, 2006).

6

Marketing and Catechetical Ministry

Navigating a Crisis

In my days as a parish catechetical leader, it was estimated that 50 percent of Catholic children were not participating in any formal Catholic faith formation via Catholic schools or parish religious education. That was in the 1990s. Today that figure is estimated at 70 percent! And if you interpret the data trends, this percentage is likely to continue increasing at an accelerating rate.

Initially, this information may dishearten those of us who love Christ and the Catholic faith. And it should sound alarm bells everywhere within the Church. Are we in crisis as a Church? It would seem that we are. However, *crisis* conveys a sense of turning point, of being at a crossroads. While the danger should be obvious, do we also see an equal or greater measure of opportunity? We should, if we are an Easter-Pentecost people.

First, what's the danger here? Simply put, the rate of active practice of Catholic faith, the rate of people identifying as Catholic, the rate of child participation in faith formation may all continue to drop, and precipitously. In a generation or two, it is conceivable that the Catholic Church in the United States could be reduced to a relative remnant of its past size and vibrancy, as has already occurred in Western Europe.

So what is the bright side of this? Where is the opportunity? There are large numbers of people who still identify as Catholic, though the connection may be very tenuous. They can be reached and engaged and brought into a deeper relationship with Christ and the Church. These people are all around us, probably in our own families. Do I think, if we do a brilliant job reaching out to and forming them, we will draw most of them into some formal relationship with a parish? That is unclear. But we will be successful with some of them—many of them, in fact! If every parish did a great job on this front, I suspect we could reengage with many tens of thousands of families across the nation. If parishes took full advantage of the opportunity for this reengagement through catechetical endeavors and *evangelized* these families, then that momentum would be contagious. These folks would bring a revitalized Catholic faith to their neighborhoods and workplaces. It could be part of a broader turnaround story for the Church as a whole!

Pope Saint John Paul II recognized that we are in an era of a *new evangelization*, calling on the Church to pay attention to the baptized-but-not-evangelized. Pope Francis has called on all in the Church to embrace an identity as missionary disciples who zealously seek to bring the good news of Jesus to the hearts and lives of others. Parish catechetical leaders have a tremendously important role to play in this vision of renewal for the Church. We need to be able to imagine a path forward for constructive action that pulls us out of despair and inertia. We need to be on fire for Christ *ourselves* and commit fully to the mission of this new evangelization. Ultimately, we will have a hand in triggering, through the Holy Spirit, not just new evangelization but a new Pentecost!

Evangelization and External Marketing

Back in the 1970s, some parishes concluded meetings by gathering in a circle to hold hands and say the Our Father—facing outward! As hokey as this might sound, I love what it symbolizes. They were saying to one another that our mission is to the world, not to ourselves or even our parishioners. (By the way, an outward-focused mission—not navel-gazing—is what young people get excited about.) That action conveyed a spirit of new evangelization and of becoming missionary disciples. Whether or not you try this on for size with your parish pastoral staff, the point remains: *Our mission is to the world.* We need to be building all facets of a parish with the foundational question, "How will this bring Christian Good News to our parishioners and the broader community?" And a second question quickly follows: "How do we get the word—the Word—out?"

Let's first look broadly at parish ministries before narrowing the focus to faith-formation ministries. In prior generations, the tried-and-somewhat-true means for marketing and promotion of events and ministries have primarily been 1) word of mouth and 2) the parish bulletin. While both these forms continue to reach the core, faithful members of the parish community, the effectiveness of these approaches has been in decline for some time because fewer people are actually engaged with the life of the parish.

A more recent addition to the mix is the parish Web site. Many parishes have paid great attention, and dedicated substantial fundds, to developing an attractive Web site. The results are admittedly mixed here. However, even with the best of Web sites, there is an undeniable limitation. "They" have to come to us, to the parish site. "They" have to seek us out. "They" need some motivation to find us. How's that working for us? Do you see the marginal, the seeker, the unchurched, knocking on your digital door? While some churches do, the fact remains that it has to happen through *their* initiative.

The expectation that a sharp Web site will effectively market the parish to the broader community is just as dangerous as the broader complacency that the Catholic Church has been so terribly guilty of over the years. "Of course, they'll get married in the Church." "At least they'll have their child baptized." Both are now in steep decline. This broader complacency is evidenced in countless ways. Here is an example to illustrate the point. When Catholics (and others) move into a neighborhood, they are often welcomed with a loaf of home-baked bread (or such) and an invitation to worship at a local Christian church. Rare is the Catholic parish that has created a culture of outreach whereby parishioners, naturally and intentionally, welcome the new family on the block, Catholic or not. Typically, we sit back. And we reap a thin harvest as a result.

The attitude that "we are the Catholic Church, and they will find us" is as un-Jesus-like as it is unwarranted today. The Gospels reveal time and time again how Jesus goes to people and meets them on their terms, on their turf, and Jesus should be our model in this and all things. Pope Francis, in emphatic and sometimes colorful ways, issued a call for us to reframe our fundamental understanding of ministry: "We should realize that missionary outreach is *paradigmatic for all the Church's activity* . . . we need to move 'from a pastoral ministry of mere conservation to a decidedly missionary pastoral ministry'" (*Joy of the Gospel*, #15, quoting from the *Aparecida Document*).

Can we agree with the premise that most people, Catholic and non-Catholic, will fail to find us? They will not just walk into our buildings. They will not check out our Web site. Why? Because the vast majority are not looking for us. This operating assumption is much safer and more accurate than the alternative. So, yes, let's make sure that the relatively few folks looking for us will find a faith community filled with Catholic goodness: joy, caring, beauty, mercy, and an experience of the sacred. And that people will see the parish Web site as attractive, intuitive, and up-to-date. But more important for younger, marginal Catholics and seekers, let's ensure that the parish will be experienced as relational, relevant, and engaging.

With that understanding in mind, let's move on to explore ways to reach people who are *not* looking to find our parish or its faith-formation ministries.

Creating a Culture of *Invite*

Evangelical churches are famous for instilling a sense of urgent responsibility in its members to reach out and invite. Invite whom? Invite *everyone*! Imagine if our Catholic parishes did the same! While our typical Catholic practice has bred a more passive culture, our theology of baptism places meaningful demands on each and every Catholic to proclaim Christ's Good News and build God's kingdom. It is our job as parish leaders, along with the Holy Spirit, to break through the hardened mind-set of passivity that has built up like plaque in our Catholic arteries.

We can accomplish this best not through guilting but rather joyfully challenging our parishioners to embrace their baptismal identity and vocation to evangelize. As we make progress in this core area, the landscape will be altered radically. We'll see the invitational power of the laity unleashed in offices, neighborhoods, online forums, and friendships throughout the world.

Someone who was sincerely interested in hearing more about the Catholic faith once asked me if I had an elevator pitch. Basically, he was asking me if I could hone my message about the Catholic faith to thirty seconds or so—the length of time people might have together in an elevator. When we think about forming a more evangelizing parish community, we should try to equip people with clear, brief talking points. Then they can find their own manner of framing the message to suit their personality and experience. Speaking from a personal faith rather than a theoretical faith will almost always be more effective.

Disrupting Insular Tendencies

Once I attended Mass at a parish whose Lenten mission series was beginning that week. The pastor followed up the mission presenter's message during Mass with an appropriate exhortation for those present to be sure to attend. The parish had a wonderful mission speaker, and the marketing effort conducted at liturgy was done very well. However, there was something missing that my evangelizing nose sniffed out instantly in the pastor's words. Can you sniff it, too?

If only those attending Mass come to the mission talks, this great mission speaker will be preaching largely to the choir. If only 20 percent of our already-active parishioners attend the mission, we need to be asking our Mass-goers to become our PR team to the rest of the parish and, perhaps more important, to the larger community. I mentioned this after Mass to the pastor and it was as if a light bulb went on in his head. He was glad for the suggestion and said he would definitely broaden the marketing strategy and enlist Mass-goers to reach out to their circle of people.

As a catechetical leader, if you can develop this knack for seeing opportunities beyond the normal, often myopic, parish-focused vision, you will be a frequent disrupter (as Pope Francis encouraged) of the status quo and a great blessing to the missionary efforts of the Church.

Open House

There was a big push in the early 2000s to market the Catholic Church through TV and radio with a campaign called "Catholics Come Home." Its effectiveness is arguable, but one conclusion is not: Inviting people to consider the Catholic faith and experience their local Catholic parish is a great idea, as long as the parish is ready for visitors. I liken it to hosting an open house when you put your home on the market. First, you clean and tidy up inside and out, perhaps add a fresh coat of paint, get some new furniture or whatever is needed to have visitors receive a great impression that may lead them to commit.

This metaphor can translate to the life of a parish. Before we go to great lengths to market our ministries thoroughly and effectively, we need to be working to get our pastoral house in order. It's a two-part equation: quality ministries *and* effective marketing. Without the two together, we are either throwing a great party that no one attends or a party we'll wish no one attended!

Old-Fashioned Community Marketing

Think about the ways people get the word out about anything in your community. And now you are starting to imagine the possibilities for how you can market your faith-formation offerings as well. Let's name just a few to get things going.

- local media (newspaper, radio, TV, municipal Web sites)
- public institutions (town hall, library, etc.)
- businesses (supermarkets, hardware stores, hair salons, doctors' offices, real-estate offices, etc.)
- mailings targeted to new residents (you can purchase this information) or full coverage of zip codes

Keep going. Make a list of venues for marketing faith-formation offerings in *your* community. Ask others to help you develop this list.

Okay, that's the *where*. Let's name the *what*—what information can be included in your marketing.

- A written blurb for media needs to
  - be relatively brief
  - cover the basics

- draw people to the Web site for more information
- incorporate at least one fun or inspirational element

- A feature piece in media (written or broadcast) can

  - afford more development about the backstory of the offering and the parish
  - provide for personal accounts and faith-sharing testimony

- A flyer, leaflet, postcard, or brochure should

  - be in color if at all possible
  - limit the number of words
  - avoid church-speak
  - be flexible to be modified to a particular audience
  - use photos and other graphics
  - include the address for the parish Web site

- A poster or placard must be

  - large enough to fit the setting
  - in color and use photos and graphics
  - tailored to speak to the audience

Signage

Not a lot needs to be said about this traditional means for marketing. However, posting signs should not be overlooked in a marketing plan. Remember that a parish is not limited to its formal, permanent signage. Consider temporary placards and billboards on multiple strategic locations on parish grounds. Lawn signs are particularly effective. Perhaps even more impactful, explore having parishioners help with marketing on their property.

Off-Site Venues

I've done a number of Theology-on-Tap (young-adult ministry) talks over the years, and many occurred in settings that created opportunities for interface with the broader community. Some were in restaurants and bars, some in parks, some in an easily accessible part of parish grounds. I remember seeing people wandering by and listening for a while, sometimes even joining the gathering. Some asked about the event and seemed genuinely interested to find out that it was a group of Catholics growing in their faith. Find ways to get parish ministry out into public settings.

Social Media

Social media is an important and quickly evolving vehicle for reaching people where they live today: online. Without a doubt, digital marketing should be a centerpiece of promoting parish ministries and faith-formation opportunities. Parishes and catechetical programs that choose to ignore this powerful means for communication and outreach do so at greater peril in the long run than they might imagine.

Following are some key principles for effective parish use of social media:

1. Have a Facebook (and other) sign-up campaign inviting *all* parishioners and others. Make it a big deal.

2. Change the profile and cover photos frequently to keep the page looking fresh.

3. *Likes* and *shares* are really important in getting the word out on Facebook. Ask parishioners and friends to *like* and *share* frequently.

4. A periodic and strategically placed *boost*, where a small fee is paid, can jump-start a campaign and broaden your reach.

Compared to traditional marketing efforts, a parish can get tremendous bang-for-its-buck doing a *boost*.

5. Post on social media with some regularity, daily if possible. Inactivity sends the wrong message about the vitality of the parish.

6. Check the page or site regularly and respond to messages in a timely manner.

7. Create security settings to be able to approve/moderate comments that are posted.

8. Monitor other parishes that have effective social-media ministry and learn and borrow from their expertise.

All these principles presume that the content being provided to visitors is good: theologically sound, interesting, timely, inspiring, and inviting. Obviously, none of this happens by accident. One or more persons will need to lead and monitor this effort. This is a perfect opportunity to enlist the help of young adults. This investment of human and material resources can pay big dividends for parishes, in terms of both growing engagement and providing content for faith formation.

Social media is, admittedly, a means of reaching parishioners in the beginning. One parish in my diocese planned their Facebook launch and created great anticipation. On their first day, over five hundred parishioners signed on. Beyond reaching parishioners, however, your social-media outreach can become a primary means for marketing also to the wider community.

Marketing Your Religious-Education Program

Most of the strategies we've covered so far for marketing parish-wide faith-formation opportunities can and should be applied to child faith-formation programs. Let's look at some insights specifically for religious-education programs.

Get Parents Involved!

Your best asset for marketing a parish faith-formation program is your parents. This works only if they are happily on board with sharing about the program (and, ideally, about the parish) with their neighbors, coworkers, etc. Very few parishes that I know of take the intentional step of asking their parents to actively promote the children's faith-formation program with others. One practical approach could be a *referral* program, where any family coming into the program can mention the existing parish family who helped to bring them in. Both the new and existing family would receive a discount on their tuition for the year. This would be a small way to highlight a big theme: the parish is looking to find more families to serve. And every parent (and child, actually) can be on the active lookout in this effort (more to fulfill their baptismal call to proclaim Jesus than to gain a tuition discount, of course).

Local Marketing for RE Programs

Recall that the majority of Catholic children are in neither a Catholic school nor a parish catechetical program. Your program's database is *not* the only market you need to reach. Your parish's database is not either. In an age of evangelization and outreach, we are required to blow the lid off that approach and market our ministry for children and families beyond our usual target audience.

Additionally, be mindful that you should be in marketing mode with your current faith-formation families all year long, not just when it is registration time. Families are making judgments continually that factor into whether they'll be back or not next year. It is sad but true that you can't take anything for granted regarding a family's continued participation in faith formation.

Two simple marketing principles should guide our efforts to reach families in the hopes of reaching and teaching as many children as possible.

- **Be broad-based.** Along with providing attractive and inviting registration material to all parish families with children of catechetical age (and following up with them), the evangelizing catechetical leader is making and tapping all possible connections to get the word out in the community. Ideally, such a leader empowers and delegates others to go out and spread the word by means of lawn signs, posters, flyers, media outlets, etc., as described earlier in this chapter. Use all possible networking and creative outreach to ensure that every family in your community knows of your excellent child faith-formation program and that they are most welcome. Consider places to give special focus for this: any sports-related activity, pediatrician offices, any place parents and children frequent, physically and online. One of the most exciting developments that I've experienced is having public-school districts cooperate in the dissemination of parish faith-formation information. Imagine if you successfully established this in your community! It is possible and can make a great difference. Reach out to your local public-school administrators/school boards to explore this.

- **Be continual.** A marketing plan to current families should consist of multiple layers. Here's an example.

  1. Let's imagine that April—May is the first time for promoting registration (with perhaps a July 1 initial deadline).

  2. July is then the time to send out a reminder to families who have not yet registered (with an August 15 deadline).

  3. After the deadline, you and others make personal calls to invite and encourage families to register. Be sure to *listen* to

parents with interest and empathy as you try to bring them into the fold. The line attributed to Theodore Roosevelt applies: "People won't care how much you know until they know how much you care."

Extending Ourselves for Christ

People are often late to register in faith-formation programs. Don't take this personally or let it frustrate you too much. Instead, create a process to discourage this trend and affirm positive actions, such as offering early-registration discounts. Even so, accept families who come in late. You can step up efforts to reach out to families even *after* the beginning of the catechetical year. Think of September and October as a second marketing season. People are back from summer break, they've gotten their children started with school, and they now are ready to look at the possibility of parish faith formation. It's a chance to make a late, ardent appeal to parish families. Without a doubt, this effort will draw in some families who would have otherwise concluded that they missed out.

Outreach and Invitation Message Template

Here is an example of an invitation to families to consider participating in your parish religious-education program.

> The Catholic parish of _____ invites you and your family to explore learning about the *Good News* of Jesus Christ and the Catholic faith. Consider growing in faith together with us! All Catholic families are encouraged to participate in this Catholic faith-formation program, and a special invitation is extended to non-Catholic families interested in learning more about faith-formation opportunities at our parish. Religious-education sessions for children are starting soon! Contact _____ at _____.

Consider including an invitation like this in the parish bulletin, on the parish or religious-education Web site, in your RE newsletter, on social media, in the local paper, etc. Do this periodically throughout the year. Families move into the community, and people's lives change, not according to our clock but in God's gracious time. Let's keep inviting folks in! Then engage them in conversation about the next best step for their family. If immediate entry into the program is not feasible, be ready to explore other options, such as home-study for the remaining weeks/months of the year or a process that parallels your existing program. (And, listen for the spiritual searching desires of the parent, possibly the more important conversation to have.)

Opportunities for marketing your religious-education program are endless: hosting "Faith-Formation Sundays" to highlight the RE program before, during, and after Masses; featuring profiles and witness statements of children, parents, and catechists in the parish bulletin; sharing witness videos on the Web site and on the Facebook page; hosting an open house, and more. Every little thing you do to promote and market your parish religious-education program is an effort to bring people closer to Christ!

Summary: Go Find the Guests

Go out, therefore, into the main roads and invite to the feast whomever you find. (Matt. 22:9, NABRE)

Jesus made it clear that he came to save all. We are stewards of *good news* meant not only for parishioners but for everyone! We must use new means to connect with people and extend ourselves beyond usual practices, knowing that most people are not looking for us.

For Reflection and Discussion

- Imagine yourself as an inactive Catholic or a seeker visiting *your* parish for the first time. What would you experience? How would it feel?

- How can parishes form all parishioners to embrace their baptismal identity and call to reach out to others and share the gospel?

Growing as a Catechetical Leader

We can become so focused on the people in front of us that we lose our peripheral vision and forget the people who aren't there. Can you develop a better vision beyond the "usual suspects"? Work with others to build a marketing strategy rooted in evangelization values.

Go to www.loyolapress.com/ECL to access the worksheet.

Suggested Action

Good leaders *overcommunicate,* internally and externally. Find ways to put this principle into practice. One example: Get the program calendar out early and by multiple means. And then provide medium- and short-range event reminders, by multiple means.

For Further Consideration

Elements of Internal Church Marketing. Chip Tudor (Chip Tudor Communications, 2014).

Go and Make Disciples: A National Plan and Strategy for Catholic Evangelization in the United States. (Washington, DC: United States Conference of Catholic Bishops, 1992, 2002).

Ministry Marketing Made Easy: A Practical Guide to Marketing Your Church Message. Yvonne Prehn (Eugene, OR: Wipf & Stock, 2012).

Teaching the Spirit of Mission Ad Gentes: Continuing Pentecost Today: A Statement of the United States Conference of Catholic Bishops. (Washington, DC: United States Conference of Catholic Bishops, June 2005).

7

Pastoral Approaches to Gathering and Engaging God's People

Everything Is Formative

Every little thing that a parish does—and I mean everything—plays a part in forming people. From the biggest event to the smallest unplanned gesture, a parish is forming its people all the time. Or, unfortunately in many cases, malforming its people. Here's an example.

A woman calls the parish to find out Mass times. The secretary handles the call with . . .

- Scenario 1: kindness, patience, and a friendly voice, inviting further engagement
- Scenario 2: hurriedness and a cold tone that causes the caller to shut down emotionally

On the surface, not much more needs to be said about this example. The phone call may further the mission of the Church, may be a missed opportunity to do so, or may actually work against the mission of the Church, which is to attract and form people for discipleship. The caller's relationship to the parish (and the Church) will affect the outcome. If the caller is an active Catholic, the call may not make much of an impact either way. If, on the other hand, he or she is a disengaged Catholic or a religious seeker, the impact of that simple exchange could be the difference between a person (and a family) ending up in a relationship with Christ and the parish or not!

It may seem like an exaggeration of what is at stake with a simple phone call about Mass times, or RE tuition, or Confirmation service hours—but it's not, at least potentially. What every member of a parish staff (and ultimately, every member of a parish) needs to understand and embrace is that every little thing we do and communicate (including through our parish facilities and grounds, our parish bulletin and digital presence, etc.) works for, or against, forming and evangelizing people.

Sweat the Small Stuff

I'd like you to stop reading for a moment and imagine your parish. Ask yourself the following: Are the bathrooms clean? Is there adequate and helpful signage? Is the temperature comfortable? Can the sound system be heard clearly? Is the Web page attractive and up-to-date? Here's one that I love to talk about: Do parishioners and staff greet people and extend a warm welcome, or at least make friendly eye contact with others?

I have experienced parishes where eye contact seems to naturally occur. (I wonder if the parish has intentionally worked on this.) I've experienced other places where God forbid that anyone look at another person, and especially a stranger. What a difference in the vibe these parishes project, especially to outsiders!

If you don't believe that everything in a parish is potentially formative about our perception of and relationship to the Church (and thus, often, by extension, our relationship to God), then I invite you to visit another parish. Better yet, go to a Christian church that is not Catholic. Look and listen. Once you are out of your element, your senses will be heightened to how things impact you. Then come back and try to see your parish with fresh eyes.

Businesses are aware of this dynamic. Go to a restaurant or a store, and try to spot all that has been put in place intentionally to draw you in, to win you over, and to make you loyal to their brand. The more you look, the more you will find: the soundtrack playing, the color scheme, the lighting, the positioning of merchandise, and the demeanor of sales personnel. In the same way, successful parishes are *intentional*. Growing, vital parishes are aware that the little things matter! They can open doors to relationships that make evangelization and formation possible.

Attentiveness and Intentionality

The successful parish—let's call it the evangelizing parish—attends with intentional care to the seemingly small things that serve the mission of Christ and the Church. Let's revisit our phone call example from above. A caring and evangelizing parish won't assume that the person calling about Mass times is a good and faithful Catholic who won't be impacted by the tone of the response. No, the successful parish will assume the opposite. Each and every call—and every other interpersonal contact of any kind—is an opportunity to impact people and their families, to win them over for Christ and bring them into the Catholic faith community of this parish.

The takeaway lesson here is that for catechetical leaders, there must be attentiveness to and intentionality about the little elements in the life and function of the program and the parish, not just the grand and important items. *Every moment, every encounter is a mission opportunity!* The small stuff determines whether we are initiating anyone into the faith.

This fact may seem daunting, but it is true. We can push away the active and engaged person (and family) with a lack of empathy and attentiveness. And, with God's grace, we can help to foster vibrant Catholic faith in a disengaged family or an unchurched person through warmth, hospitality, and a welcoming attitude. It's our choice.

Hold on to these foundational principles as we now delve into practices in catechetical leadership for engaging people effectively. Let's look at different types of *gatherings* with parishioners and people exploring faith.

Encounters

I define *encounters* as individual or small-group gatherings that are not scheduled. Encounters can be drop-in visits to your office or chance encounters on the parish grounds or elsewhere, including the grocery store, for example. Just because something is not scheduled doesn't mean it's not important. The happenstance encounter and the intentional but unscheduled drop-in visit by another can be the Holy Spirit at work. How we receive the person can make all the difference in whether we are cooperating with the Spirit or serving to block the grace of the Spirit.

Let's say that during a faith-formation session, you have a scheduled appointment in ten minutes or you are busy with responsibilities. It is entirely appropriate to communicate this to the person(s) with whom you are having a nonemergency encounter. But first, convey a genuine gladness to see them! The person you are scheduled with deserves respect and promptness from you. Communicating this allows the person in front of you to work within your time constraint.

Aside from having a pressing appointment, a catechetical leader should try to be "all in" for the impromptu encounter. It may feel as though this encounter is an intrusion into the planned course of your day. But do your best to make the internal adjustment within yourself to see this moment as a blessing, as a moment of opportunity to follow the promptings of the Holy Spirit, and as a chance to do something beautiful for God. An adage in ministry circles goes like this: "I used to have constant interruptions from my ministry. Now I can see that the interruptions *are* my ministry."

For all such encounters, strive for the following:

- Find a welcoming setting for conversation.
- If you are in your office, avoid sitting behind your desk (which communicates power and inaccessibility) if possible.
- Offer hospitality (hang up their coat, offer a refreshment).
- Avoid looking at your watch or the clock or otherwise seeming impatient or distracted.
- Pay attention to your body language and affect.
- Listen carefully for the stated and unstated hopes and needs of the person, and put the other person first.
- When needed, find a path to a constructive conclusion, including a possible follow-up appointment or referral to others.

You are called to serve the person in front of you in the name of Jesus Christ and the Church. It can take great mental energy to be truly present to the other person, especially when it was not in your plans. See the person before you, in any given moment, as the most important person in the world . . . indeed, as the face of Jesus. If you can develop this pastoral discipline, you are, as the Bible says, not far from the reign of God.

One catechetical leader I know set up a comfortable space to serve coffee and flavored creamers and little treats. She made it known that parishioners were welcome to drop by for coffee and a visit (if she were available) or to do a little reading from the catechetical and spiritual resources there. It was always "open house" and with personal care. What great availability!

Having said all this, let me offer a caveat: A catechetical leader has work to do. There are expectations of the pastor to fulfill, calls to return, deadlines to meet. Pastoral presence should be a high value, but it needs to be held in appropriate tension with other values of the role. There is no recipe for finding the perfect balance here. I simply suggest that you keep people as the first priority, as Pope Francis suggests in *Joy of the Gospel*. Be fully *with* people (and not distracted) when you are able. When you are not able to give people your time and focused attention, simply be honest, explain the situation, and look for another opportunity to be with them.

What matters most when we are relating to another person? You might be surprised to learn that the vast majority of the information received interpersonally is not through words at all but through facial expression and vocal intonation. Pay attention to your affect, because it matters more than you would ever imagine.

You are always the face of the parish, the face of the Church—no matter where, no matter when. You may not want this. You may feel unworthy to be perceived as the face of the Church. However, it is part and parcel of the role of catechetical leadership. Humbly accept this privileged position. Pray for the grace to represent the Church, in your planned moments of ministry and in the surprises.

Appointments

Planned appointments are generally easier to navigate because we have a chance to prepare our thoughts and words. We often know the purpose for meeting and the personality (or personalities) of those with whom we're meeting, which can give us a measure of confidence and focus. Leaders who prefer structure will feel good about a planned segment of the day and getting things accomplished.

Here are some particular insights for the planned appointment.

- Be prompt or a bit early, whether the appointment is on your turf or elsewhere.

- Come prepared with the information needed and the desire to meet the needs of the other person(s).

- Be focused on the purpose of the meeting, though also intuitive and flexible as needed.

- Be mindful of the time frame for this meeting, for everyone's sake.

- Generally, avoid scheduling appointments back-to-back, in case a bit more time is needed.

- Meet off-site when appropriate, especially with someone who is not very "churchy."

Intercessory Prayer and Ministry

Because you're a catechetical leader, parishioners will share all sorts of difficult (and joyful) news with you and often ask you to pray for them. Here are some suggestions for responding pastorally.

- Reverence these occasions as opportunities for profound grace.

- Gauge whether they are seeking some pastoral care through their sharing.

- Ask if they would like the prayer circle to be enlarged to include parts of the community or the entire parish.

- If you promise to pray for them, stop everything and do it immediately after the call or e-mail.

- Start a notebook where you keep track of people's prayer requests.

- Develop a practice of bringing these intentions regularly before the Blessed Sacrament in church.

- Find ways to check in with the person to learn how things are going.

- Consider not just promising to pray *for* but also to pray *with* the person—in the moment.

- Gather together as parish leaders to pray for these intentions.

Guidelines for Effective Communication

Much of your interrelating with parishioners may occur by telephone and e-mail. Here are a few pointers for how to make these engagements constructive to the mission of Jesus and the Church.

Phone Calls

- Answer every call with a pleasant professional tone and sound glad to be talking with the person. The more difficult the situation or person, the more important this is. The tenor for the conversation is established in the first few seconds. (Try smiling as you answer or make a phone call. It will help with this!)

- Even more than in person, *active listening skills* are vital.

  ○ Give people the time and space they need to share their thoughts and feelings.

  ○ Give periodic verbal cues that you are "with" people.

  ○ Make sure they are feeling heard, understood, and respected by reframing and sharing back some of what they are saying.

  ○ Acknowledge the value of their good intentions (prayer requests), and affirm them whenever possible.

- Patiently look for opportunities to contribute information and your perspective—to what, ultimately, should be a dialogue.

- If there is tension or disagreement, take care not to sharpen your tone or raise your volume.

- Consider making notes to document matters discussed, or follow up with an e-mail to summarize a conversation.

- Return phone calls as soon as possible. Treat them as a higher priority than e-mails, in general.

- Leave messages that give brief, pertinent information, and include a personal touch when possible.

Whether on the phone or in person, I have found you can say almost anything to anyone and have it go relatively well—as long as you convey respect and caring. Tone is key! Let people know you're on their side, even if you disagree with them or can't give them what they want. Enter into any engagement (in person, on the phone, or in e-mail) with a desire to say yes whenever possible and the courage to say no when necessary. But when there is a no, always look for alternative possibilities . . . a creative "third way." Often this ends up being a win-win for all parties.

E-mails, Texts, and Tweets

- Respond to parishioner messages in a timely manner, within twenty-four hours, if possible.
- Consider whether a phone call would be more helpful and warrant the additional time that a call typically takes.
- Be as personable as the medium and the particular dynamics allow.
- Assume the best (and not the worst) in the person's intentions. Don't be cynical or defensive.
- Take special care to communicate clearly and with sufficient thoroughness.
- Avoid any language that could be reasonably interpreted as sarcastic or snarky.
- Read your e-mails, texts, and tweets carefully before sending them, to ensure they are professional communications. Wait an hour (or a day) before sending if in doubt or if the subject matter is highly charged.

- Always consider what e-mail, text, and Twitter conversations should be retained, either digitally or in hard copy. Consider the long-term effects, and if in doubt, retain, at least for a while.

E-mailing, texting, and tweeting are tremendous modes for ministry communication. They are ways to keep in touch with individuals and groups that efficiently further a discussion and convey information. I very much appreciate that they provide a paper trail of sorts, which is helpful for recall and for holding myself and others accountable. Utilize these amazing tools to enhance your ability to be both relational and productive.

A note of caution regarding e-mails, texts, and tweets: They can be misinterpreted, as you may already know. They don't contain the nuance available in face-to-face and telephone encounters. As my etiquette suggestions imply, be careful. Communicating via digital media can, unfortunately, turn a small misunderstanding into a crisis. And remember, you are creating a paper trail for the receiver, too. Your communication might be shared with others and used against you. Craft your messages with this in mind. Being clear and courteous is always the way to go.

Consider any digital-media messaging as a ministry opportunity beyond the particular initial purpose. I call this having "ministerial peripheral vision." This vision, which sees beyond the immediate and is open to the Holy Spirit, should apply to all encounters but seems especially suited to social-media messaging. Ask yourself these questions: How can I invite this person into a deeper relationship with Christ and the parish? What underlying issues can be surfaced for care and remediation? Whom else can I connect this person to? What resource Web link would be helpful to share?

I want to stress the value of being caring in the tone and content of your messages. I'm amazed at how often my little messages expressing particular interest or concern, sharing from my life, or simply well-wishing have made a great difference on my receiver's end. Take the time to be kind and personal. It is the best investment of an extra minute you can make, for you are investing in relationships. And always consider adding a last reply that conveys something much needed in our society today—*graciousness*. Simple graciousness can be a real difference maker in our evangelizing mission. (Remember, it's the small things that often matter the most.)

Being a Punching Bag Is Not in Your Job Description

When it comes to handling difficult situations, we can choose one of the following three options:

- Assertiveness—appropriate, respectful, but firm conveyance of one's position and values
- Aggressiveness—undue use of power and force to confront and quell opposition
- Abusiveness—use of some manner of violence upon another

Obviously, assertiveness is the only appropriate posture of these three options when it comes to pastoral ministry. Because a catechetical leader has a degree of power/authority inherent in the position, aggressiveness is never an appropriate mode for relating to parishioners. Assertiveness, meanwhile, is a valuable asset and a quality that communicates confidence in one's convictions and in one's self. Dignity, humility, and moral courage are qualities of the assertive person. Indeed, asserting proper values for the betterment of others is generous and loving. On many occasions in the Gospels, we find Jesus displaying holy assertiveness in the face of derision and abuse. He models for us the gentleness and strength required for leadership.

There may be occasions when someone will act with aggression toward you in your role. And you may even find yourself the recipient of abusive language. First, realize that most often such behavior is not primarily about you or your ministry. There are frequently underlying issues and stresses causing the person to act out in such ways. The ideal (though not always easy) response is to feel compassion for the person. If you are able to work through initial aggressive behavior or abusive language, you may be able to help the person get to a better place and even experience the heart of Christ in his or her encounter with you. Saying a silent prayer in those moments is always a good idea.

Do not feel, however, that you are required by your ministerial role to be subjected to any sustained degree of abusive language or aggressive behavior. In such instances, you should feel entirely free to disengage. In the case of abusive speech, for example, it is appropriate to express sentiments such as, "I'm happy to have a conversation with you, but at the moment I'm being shouted at and demeaned. We can continue this at a later time, perhaps as early as tomorrow. But it needs to be a respectful conversation."

Gathering God's People: Speaking Their Language

Do you know what CCD stands for? The correct answer is: Confraternity of Christian Doctrine. This title was used for decades to refer to faith formation for Catholic children attending public schools. Do you know what decade this acronym officially went away? The 1960s. Do you know what decade it will stop being used entirely? Me neither. This is just one example of what one might refer to as "insider" language or "church talk"—words, phrases, and acronyms that are used regularly by Catholics in ministry but are not familiar to the average person. Whenever you gather God's people and speak to them, use language familiar to the average person, and avoid churchy jargon. Catholic vocabulary can be introduced later as people become more and more immersed in the Catholic way of life. Words really do matter, so pay attention to the terminology you choose.

For example, if the parish faith-formation commission or RE advisory board is gathering, there's no problem referring to it as a meeting. Meeting language is fine for internal leadership *business* gatherings. When, however, we're talking about something relating to parents, parishioners, and others and our purpose has an explicit or implicit intent to catechize-evangelize, I urge you to move toward softer and, frankly, more apt language such as gathering, session, morning (afternoon, evening) of reflection, forum, learning or discussion or small-community group, etc. After all, who really likes going to a meeting?

Regarding child faith-formation programming, since we are moving away from a purely academic approach, it would be more appropriate to refer to "sessions" instead of "classes" and "participants" or "young people" instead of "students." Catechesis should not resemble merely another subject in their school curriculum. The last thing children will want is to go to one more class. It is for this reason that I'm not a fan of the moniker "Parish School of Religion."

Adult Formation Gatherings

While it is important not to refer to adult faith-formation gatherings as "classes," it is even more crucial that such sessions do not have the *feel* of a class. Few adults will be excited, after a long day at work or home, to come for a class of any sort. As you and those with whom you collaborate design catechist training sessions, parent evenings of reflection, or an adult formation series, consider the goals and objectives, the content to be shared, and the process that will be utilized. Don't overlook environment and setup. The design should take into consideration the circumstances and human needs of your learners and where they are in faith development. Good design is always attentive and respectful to people. This applies to both required sessions and optional ones.

Parent Gatherings

Let's focus on parent gatherings for a moment (see more on *parents* in chapter 9). In today's reality it is entirely proper to see these as opportunities for evangelization more than catechesis. Sure, some of your parents are already evangelized and would optimally benefit from a rich and advanced catechetical experience. However, typically and unfortunately, most of our Catholic parents are more appropriately candidates for either initial invitation to a personal faith in Jesus Christ (evangelization) or a return to an active and personal faith in Christ (re-evangelization).

Those parents who are evangelized can still benefit from a vibrant kerygmatic message of Catholic faith . . . an *evangelizing catechesis*. But providing advanced catechesis to unevangelized parents will only deepen their sense of disheartenment and disconnect from the Church. Here are some elements to weave into parent formation sessions.

- Comfortable setting and hospitality that create a sense of safety, welcome, and joy
  - Rich prayer experience that is not rushed or perfunctory, with inclusion of Scripture, silence, and reflection, Catholic liturgical symbols, art and sacramentals, and possibly music
  - Catholic faith content that meets the goal(s) of the session and meets people where they are—connecting faith with life through in-person proclamation, teaching, and clips of engaging videos
  - Faith testimonials provided by parent-peers through witnessing accounts and panel discussion

- ○ Table conversation and/or one-to-one sharing woven throughout that engages parents and fosters a sense of connection and participation
- ○ Invitation to a deepening of relationship to God, Church, parish, and family grounded in Jesus that feels loving and not judgmental
- ○ Resources provided for their faith enrichment
- ○ Resources provideed for family faith enrichment

Having different voices contribute to the session is helpful. Infusing these sessions with energy and humor is tremendously effective in breaking down barriers, drawing people in, and opening them up to grace. For better or worse, these people are not, on the whole, very churchy. We are smart to avoid sounding too churchy ourselves or we risk putting them into a disaffected mode. Relating to them on their terms is a key element in the evangelization process. Our time with parents is so limited and precious. Do we want to insist they jump the gap that lies between them and the Church, or do we want to spend that time building a bridge?

As for catechist meetings and adult faith-formation offerings, while there might be a value in visiting evangelizing themes, these gatherings can and should take active parishioners deeper into the rich intellectual and spiritual tradition of Catholicism. Hopefully, you and the parish staff have some ability to lead such sessions, at least in part. Regarding your pastor and other parish leaders, consider their strengths and provide them opportunities to draw upon them. Additionally, the good news is that never before has there been such an outstanding array of adult catechetical resources available. Many excellent resources are available for you to use in a variety of formats. Consult your diocesan catechetical office and publishing partners about such resources.

Remember that today's learning style demands that we engage people. They have little patience for passive formation, and we can lose them relatively quickly. Find different ways to change things up throughout a gathering. It could be as simple as providing ten minutes of input and then having them discuss a couple of questions at their table, and then repeating this process. Also consider some quiet reflection time mixed in for the introverts in the room.

Ministry Meetings

Sometimes we gather for what can appropriately be called a meeting. Let's use your faith-formation commission or religious-education board as our example, and name helpful facets to keep in mind.

- Create an agenda in advance of the meeting. A good practice is to invite suggested items from others and include an estimated length of time for each item. This helps to keep a meeting on track.
- Provide refreshments and create a comfortable environment.
- Start the meeting promptly and honor the concluding time that was set. Respect people's time.
- Invite the presence of the Holy Spirit through meaningful prayer. Some faith sharing should occur. (Using the upcoming Sunday Gospel for all parish meetings can unify all ministries in the centrality of Sunday Eucharist.)
- Facilitate the meeting. Whether you or a chairperson, an effective facilitator
  - has a feel for group dynamics;
  - knows how to manage discussion, allowing people a chance to speak but also reining them in as needed;
  - keeps the discussion moving on task and on time; and
  - clarifies and summarizes effectively.
- Develop notes of essential information and decisions made, to be shared in a timely manner after the meeting.

A healthy ministry group is a learning community. Consider as a group how a formational piece can be woven into its work. This could mean reading and discussing a key church document or book, a chapter at a time. Or perhaps the group can participate in a brief learning or service activity, regularly or semi-regularly.

Summary: The Face of Christ

Jesus, looking at him, loved him and said . . . "follow me." (Mark 10:21)

Jesus' ministry was characterized by personal encounters that invited people into relationship with the Father. Our ministry calls us to be pastorally present to those whom we encounter. Our gatherings, whether evangelizing-catechesis events or internally oriented meetings, should be designed to foster conversion and deepen discipleship to Jesus.

For Reflection and Discussion

- In what ways does your ministry role allow you to share about your journey of discipleship and invite others to reflect and share about theirs?

- Look at the flow of a recent or upcoming gathering. What can be done to make it less perfunctory and more potentially transformative? How can your formation events be more "from the heart" and "to the heart"?

Growing as a Catechetical Leader

How are your vocal intonation and body language as you relate to people? The camera doesn't lie, as they say. Watch and listen to yourself on videotape to get a more accurate gauge of your affect and how you come across. You can also practice in front of the mirror.

Go to www.loyolapress.com/ECL to access the worksheet.

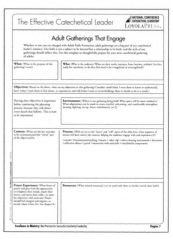

Suggested Action

Use the fourfold prayer structure of *naming, praising, thanking,* and *asking* God to develop prayer at meetings and other gatherings that convey both a theological coherence and a heartfelt spirituality.

For Further Consideration

A Church on the Move: 52 Ways to Get Mission and Mercy in Motion. Joe Paprocki (Chicago: Loyola Press, 2016).

How to Form Families with Learning Centers. Paul Canavese (Alameda, CA: The Pastoral Center, 2016).

Leading Small Groups with a Purpose. Steve Gladen (Grand Rapids, MI: Baker Books, 2012).

Rebuilt: Awakening the Faithful, Reaching the Lost, and Making Church Matter. Michael White and Tom Corcoran (Notre Dame, IN: Ave Maria Press, 2012).

8

Catechesis and Liturgy
Belong Together

Depth Perspective

Have you ever stood too close to something to see it? When you step back and get some perspective on any large work of art, for example, all of a sudden you start to see what the artist wanted you to see. Catholicism is like a massive mosaic masterpiece. It takes up the height and breadth of a large wall. It is beautiful . . . magnificent, in fact. But like a visitor to an art museum, one needs to step back—way back—to be able to grasp its magnificence and perceive its effect as a whole.

My sense is that what we, as catechetical leaders, have done over the generations is give our learners lots and lots (and lots) of Catholic mosaic tiles. We hand them pieces of information, tiles that relate to one aspect of our faith or another, and invite learners to study the tile and come to understand it. One tile could be a Scripture passage, one about a saint. Another tile is a doctrine, and another is a devotion.

This approach can be effective if we are training children, teens, and adults to compete in Catholic trivia competitions. However, this is obviously not the objective of faith formation. Our goal is not simply to stuff the heads of children, teenagers, and adults with lots of information. We endeavor to put people in touch with the broad sweep of history—salvation history—that climaxes in Jesus' life, Death, and

Resurrection and how this reveals a God who is profoundly invested and personally engaged in our lives. Our goal, ultimately, is to shepherd people into personal and saving relationship with God and have them experience grace in their living of Christian discipleship and Catholic faith. Each mosaic tile of Catholicism is beautiful in its own right and worthy of varying degrees of exploration. But I suggest that we *continually* refer our learners back to the big picture of Catholic faith as we introduce particular tiles of our faith.

The Church's Call to Liturgical Formation

The Church teaches us that the key to entering into the "big picture" of the Paschal Mystery of Jesus is to make sure that our faith formation brings catechesis and liturgy together into a seamless experience.

> Catechesis is intrinsically linked with the whole of liturgical and sacramental activity. . . . [S]acramental life is impoverished and very soon turns into hollow ritualism if it is not based on serious knowledge of the meaning of the sacraments, and catechesis becomes intellectualized if it fails to come alive in the sacramental practice. (*Catechesi Tradendae*, #23)

In fact, one of the Six Tasks of Catechesis, mentioned frequently throughout this series, is "Liturgical Education." The *National Directory for Catechesis* reminds us that this task calls us to "teach about the form and meaning of the liturgy and the sacraments and help individuals prepare their minds and hearts to enter into these mysteries of our faith" (#20).

Seeing Prayer Differently

As a new DRE, I noticed something curious (a more polite word than *dysfunctional*) about the formation our parish children were experiencing. We were doing a good job teaching them about prayer.

However, we were doing a not-so-hot job of praying *with* them. Coming in with fresh eyes, I could see how unfortunate this was and wanted to fix it.

I began to contextualize parish faith-formation ministry with the catechists, helping them to see it within the bigger picture of what we were trying to accomplish. This was the early 1990s, and we didn't yet have the benefit of the *General Directory for Catechesis* (1995). I found myself drawing from a surprisingly oldie-but-goodie resource: the *Baltimore Catechism*, which begins with the question *Why did God make you?* Why do we exist? What are we doing here and what's the point of it all? These are questions that invite us to "back up the truck" to the ultimate big-picture questions of life and meaning. The rote response from some older catechists was verbatim from the *Baltimore Catechism*: "God made me to know Him, to love Him, and to serve Him in this world, and to be happy with Him forever in the next."

This is a really good answer to the big-picture question, to the great existential search for meaning and purpose in our lives. There are three elements to consider for our life here on earth:

1. To know God—which is what we often associate with evangelization and catechesis
2. To love God—our prayer and worship
3. To serve God—living virtuous lives where we love and care for others out of love for God

On one level there is the linear sequence:

We must first come to know God before we have any chance to love and serve him. How can we love anyone until we have come to know him or her? This makes perfect sense. In this way, it can be said that catechetical ministry is a *foundational* ministry, a necessary core piece to forming disciples.

But on a deeper level, it quickly becomes apparent that a linear sequencing of these elements is too simplistic. There is a dynamic relationship among these three categories. Any of them can be the entry point into life in Christ. And the progression will vary depending on the person and his or her experience and circumstance.

For example: Our participation in social-justice ministries (caring for the hungry and needy, visiting the lonely and imprisoned, etc.) can get us in touch with the mystery of suffering and grace and our inadequacy in ministering to others. Such experiences then draw us into a desire for prayer and a hunger for the Eucharist as sources of nourishment we need to be able to bring God's grace and healing to others. Then, our experience in prayer and liturgy and sacramental life instills in us a desire to enter more deeply into knowing our God.

Whatever the path for growing in our knowledge of God, our love of God, and our service in God's name, we should see it as a dynamic, lifelong journey. We loop back and continue to cycle ever more deeply into the mystery of God and our invitation to live in his love, for the salvation and good of all.

This big-picture approach to our faith was a helpful initial element of formation of catechists under my care and leadership. It helped those wonderful catechists broaden their understanding of what we were attempting to accomplish, in God's grace, with our students. In this larger context, prayer was not simply something that needed to be conducted before getting to the meat of the session. Prayer was not at all like a catechetical Pledge of Allegiance. Prayer, rather, went to the heart of the matter and was an integral component in holistic formation for Christian discipleship and Catholic lifestyle.

Liturgical Formation: Catechists First, Then Children

After I reminded my catechists about the big-picture approach to faith formation, we spent a year praying well as a community of catechists. I wanted them to "get it" before I asked them to implement prayer with the children in their care. We replaced the perfunctory hoop-jumping prayer at the beginning of class with meaningful prayer experiences. Following are some elements I used for catechist meetings and other gatherings:

- the thoughtful design of a liturgical environment, such as sacred symbols (cross/crucifix, water, candle, etc.), seasonal color(s), lectionary, art
- the reverent inclusion of ritual actions (the sign of the cross, processing with lectionary, etc.)
- Scripture ritually and reverently proclaimed
- an invitation to reflection and sharing (small group and large group)
- the integration of silence, patient pacing, and music

- an invitation to petitionary prayer as well as communal prayers, such as the Lord's Prayer and other traditional prayers
- a sharing of a sign of peace

What do these elements remind you of? If you said Catholic liturgy (or the Mass), you'd be right! We have a public manner of praying as Catholics, structured and ritualized, that is ancient, rich, and beautiful. Our liturgical tradition offers us a graced treasury from which to draw as we seek to provide experiences of prayer to any group in any setting, be it catechist formation or otherwise.

Prayers of the Church

We have for each day (and every movement of the day) the gift of the Liturgy of the Hours as a structured means of praying as the Universal Church. The Liturgy of the Hours can be a great source for building a prayer experience that forms people in both the ancient and the universal qualities of the Church. This prayer resource is not just for clergy. It is available to all Catholic people, and it is readily accessible online from a variety of sources, such as Universalis (www.universalis.com); Divine Office (https://divineoffice.org); eBreviary (www.ebreviary.com); USCCB (www.usccb.org); iBreviary (www.ibreviary.org); and others. Consider pulling even a portion of it into a session with catechists and young people. In doing so, you will expose them to a very Catholic, liturgical way of prayer as a community.

Catechetical leaders do not need to reinvent the wheel! You don't need to be all that creative or search for themes for Lent and Easter that involve caterpillars and butterflies. The Church already has its theme, and it involves the Cross and the empty tomb. Likewise, every Mass already has its theme named: the paschal mystery of Jesus Christ. All else falls within this context.

Look to the seasons and feasts as you build liturgical prayer experiences. Draw from the readings in the Lectionary for that day or the upcoming Sunday. (These can be found at www.usccb.org/bible/readings.) Incorporate the happenings in our world or in your community as well. Provide opportunities for silence, introspection, and sharing that are not readily possible at Mass. Allow for more firsthand entry into the world of Catholic symbol and ritual so that participants may truly experience our incarnational and sacramental faith. Creatively integrate our rich Catholic prayer tradition into your local setting and the particular moment. In doing so, you will be both praying well and forming well. The ancient Latin maxim (attributed to Saint Prosper of Aquitaine) *Lex orandi, lex credendi*, reminds us "The law of praying is the law of believing."

In summation regarding the public prayer of the Church, we must form catechists to 1) appreciate the integral place prayer and liturgy hold within the catechetical endeavor, and 2) lead prayer comfortably and fruitfully within the Catholic liturgical tradition when praying in any group setting, be it with children or adults.

Personal Prayer

As with everything Catholic, ours is a "both/and" effort. We form people for participation in the *public* (liturgical) prayer life of the Church to strengthen both them and the parish. We also form people for a *personal* prayer life for ongoing conversion, virtue, and sanctification.

There is much to be said about private prayer from a Catholic perspective. Traditional prayers such as the Our Father, Hail Mary, and others have an esteemed place in our faith and are essential in the life of every Catholic. Knowing prayers by heart is a blessing for a lifetime of Catholic life. Do not shy away from having an expectation that such prayers be known and carried within your learners' hearts. Spontaneous prayer has a very special place, too, in Catholic life. This is more essential as we increasingly recognize the need to form people for a personal (not to be confused with *private*) relationship with God and to live as intentional followers of Christ Jesus. As you lead, help children and adults grow comfortable with prayer that is as accessible as conversation with one's closest friend (who also happens to be our transcendent Creator and God).

It is part of human nature to be more inclined to talk than to listen. Hence, emphasis needs to be given to the *listening* side of the prayer equation. Inculcate a valuing of silence, of surrendering the agenda in prayer, and learning to be open to communication beyond human words. In essence, this is introducing learners to the mystical prayer tradition of *contemplation*. Contemplative prayer is one of the great gifts of Catholicism and one that has been underutilized. In a world that has never moved faster, when our attention span continues to dwindle and our collective anxiety continues to rise, giving children and adults practice in prayer that is patient, still, and open to the movement of God may be initially challenging. However, over time it can become a tremendous gift and blessing in their life. Help your people to hunger for holy solitude and to embrace sacred silence. I have seen this happen in the lives of people of all ages, and it can change them to their core!

Implementing Liturgical Prayer

During my first year as a parish DRE, in addition to giving my catechists liturgical formation and prayer experiences, I began preparing them for what was to come next year. I was empowering them to lead liturgical prayer experiences each week with the children in their care.

Reactions ranged from "I'm excited!" to "I quit!" Actually, only a small handful didn't feel up to the task in the end. It was so satisfying to see how catechists came to embrace and delight in their roles as liturgical prayer leaders with the children. (By the time I left my role at the parish, several catechists assured me that our Lectionary-based liturgical prayer would continue—whether my successor wanted it or not. Indeed, it did live on.)

Since Lectionary-based liturgical prayer is grounded in Scripture, my first move was to purchase enough Lectionaries to fully serve our program. I chose Lectionaries that were of aesthetic value. They cost more, but as Saint Thomas Aquinas taught, grace builds upon nature. What better place to invest than in the word of God? I wanted the children in our program to know, in ways they could see and touch, that the word of God is important and beautiful and central to Catholic faith. Aesthetics matter, and photocopied Scripture passages have no place in faith formation . . . ever.

We also provided a Lectionary-based resource to help catechists understand the readings for the upcoming Sunday. The resource I used assisted them in explaining the readings and inviting the children to reflect on the word proclaimed from their perspective. It was important for our children to be actively engaged in the reflection on the word proclaimed, not just talked at by the catechist. We focused mostly on the Gospel (due to time constraints and accessibility to the other readings), though exceptions were made on occasion.

Another resource for liturgical prayer is *lectio divina*, or "divine reading." Increasingly, versions of *lectio divina* are being used with learners of all ages as a way to engage actively with Scripture and go deeper in reflection and application to one's life. This is a wonderful development, and all Catholics should be exposed to this scriptural prayer practice. However, be sure that sufficient time is available to do this well. If *lectio divina* has to be rushed, it is not all that helpful.

Elements of the liturgical prayer experience our catechists developed centered on the Gospel and the liturgical season (and special feasts). They included the liturgical environment, ritual actions (drawn from the Mass), music (both for singing and reflection), and recited and spontaneous prayer. Also consider inviting participants (perhaps one each session) to include something personal and holy in their lives in the prayer space (a baseball card from Grandpa, a rosary from Grandma, etc.).

Catholic faith formation always should have its eye on how it forms people into the praying life of the Church and, in particular, the Mass. One of the blessings in the prayer approach we established was that the parish (in every session of every grade) was forming children intentionally for active participation in the community's liturgical action. Those children attending Mass on Sunday were prepared in a local, age-appropriate setting to have an enriched experience of the Mass. They could lean over to their mom or dad and say, "We heard this reading in RE." And for those children not attending Mass regularly, the prayer they experienced each session was the closest they would get to a liturgical experience that week. It was a "win" regardless.

Liturgical Sensibility: Being Hungry . . . Staying Catholic

We've all watched the phenomenon play out in our parishes, and even in our own families: young people raised diligently in the Catholic faith, even in active families of faith, who quickly and easily jettison Catholicism for another faith or no faith practice at all. It is one of the great sources of heartache for any of us who know the profound blessing that is being Catholic.

I've ministered in the shadow of Willow Creek Community Church, the mother church of modern non-denominationalism in the United States. I've attended such churches to learn what might draw young people away from the Catholic faith. While evangelical church services have a way of engaging and inspiring, many of them lack a liturgical form and structure—at least in the traditional Catholic sense.

My strongly held conviction is that if we can form our children really well liturgically, we will have helped to inoculate them, to a degree, against dropping their Catholic faith. Or, if they try on other forms of Christianity (or even non-faith), this "sensibility" within them is likely to foster a hunger for more—the "going deep" potentiality of Catholic liturgy, the Catholic sacramental imagination, as some call it—at some future point in their life journey. As adults, they will be more likely to find their way home.

The Eucharist

Having a sense of the Eucharist as the most intimate experience of God's love and Jesus' *real presence* will tether those we teach to the Catholic faith. Having the sense that the Eucharist is food for the journey of discipleship will beckon them frequently to the table where we feast.

Recalling the mosaic metaphor from earlier in the chapter, the Eucharist is not merely another tile. As "source and summit of the Christian life" (*Dogmatic Constitution on the Church* or *Lumen Gentium,* 11), the Eucharist may be understood as the centerpiece that completes the Catholic mosaic. It could also be understood as the adhesive substance that holds the entire work together, allowing the many tiles to reveal the grand Word-Made-Flesh narrative. The Eucharist can never be relegated to a grade or a lesson. Catholicism makes sense only when the Eucharist makes sense. *It needs to permeate the entire catechetical vision of your parish.*

Family Liturgical Formation

It is all well and good to form children to have a Catholic liturgical sensibility and to value the Mass. But what about their parents? As catechetical leaders, we need to find ways to form parents to grow in their understanding of the grace and power in the Eucharist and eucharistic liturgy. There are wonderful resources out there to help us in this effort at church. But we can also bring a liturgical sensibility *home* for parents and children to experience together.

One such approach is to provide the Lectionary readings to parents (each month or quarter) and a resource to assist them in unpacking the Scriptures with their children. Over time, and with repeated, consistent encouragement, you can build a culture at your parish in which parents feel invited to pray the Lectionary readings as a family at home. Folks will know that this is highly valued, and many families will embrace the opportunity to make this kind of prayer a part of their domestic church.

The approach I favor is to ask families to gather around the word of God on Sunday evening, after (in the ideal) having heard it preached earlier in the weekend. Encourage them to create a prayer space in the home (ideally, permanent), a place where a Bible is enthroned with a crucifix, and other faith symbols and items meaningful to the family are laid out. In this sacred space of the home, the family can reflect on God's word and consider its implications for how they should live that week. In essence, they are creating their own family ritual prayer, their own liturgical experience. They can include recited prayers and other liturgical elements as suit them while also tethering their family to the larger Church.

Components of a Holistic Formation Approach

Are we forming children to know their faith? Are we forming children to live in homes rooted in Catholic faith? Are we forming children to be comfortable with and joyful in their participation in the worshipping and broader life of the parish?

Note the triangle in the diagram above. Each corner of this triangle represents an essential dimension to holistic, integrated faith formation. Remember, our goal is not solely that people have a Catholic identity or that they are going to Mass. Our goal, the goal of the Church, is much bigger: to form people for passionate and intentional discipleship to Jesus Christ and a robust Catholic lifestyle . . . both inside the triangle and beyond, out in the world.

Summary: The Bread That Holds Us Together

Then he took the bread, said the blessing, broke it, and gave it to them, saying, "This is my body, which will be given for you; do this in memory of me." (Luke 22:19, NABRE)

Spend time entering this so-familiar narrative of Jesus' *radical* self-giving again. The Eucharist is the epicenter of grace, organically intertwined with the saving Cross. Catechesis and liturgy belong together. We cannot form people too much or too well in the Eucharist, or in the liturgy that provides it. People who know and love God will yearn for personal times of divine intimacy. Families who understand and experience the blessings the Church gives us through public liturgy will far more likely be Catholic in a deep and lasting way.

For Reflection and Discussion

- Do you gravitate to the sweeping mosaic that is Catholicism? Or do you tend to zero in on individual tiles? How can you keep focus on the larger context in your leadership and teaching style?

- What is prayer like in your ministries? In RE sessions, at adult gatherings, before meetings? Does it feel hurried and flat? Is it impactful for people . . . and potentially transformative?

Growing as a Catechetical Leader

What is your formational grounding in the organic symbolic elements of Christianity (cross, water, oil, fire, etc.) and the ritual gestures (e.g., sign of the cross), and how can it be enriched? Consider how to better form catechists in core symbols and rituals of our faith, which will help catechists shift away from an emphasis on peripheral or non-Christian elements.

Go to www.loyolapress.com/ECL to access the worksheet.

Suggested Action

Move away from overreliance on paper in prayer experiences. Find ways to make prayer more reflective and less a reading exercise. Select an upcoming meeting or gathering to try out a richer, more patient, more organically Catholic-Christian prayer experience.

For Further Consideration

From Mass to Mission: Understanding the Mass and Its Significance for Our Christian Children. Joyce Donahue (Chicago: Liturgy Training Publications, 2016).

Great Is the Mystery: Encountering the Formational Power of Liturgy. Joe Paprocki and D. Todd Williamson (Chicago: Liturgy Training Publications, 2012).

How to Talk to Children about the Mass. Tom Quinlan (New London, CT: Twenty-Third Publications, 2017).

Liturgy and the New Evangelization: Practicing the Art of Self-Giving Love. Timothy P. O'Malley (Collegeville, MN: Liturgical Press, 2014).

A Liturgical Companion to the Documents of the Second Vatican Council. Joyce Donahue et al. (Chicago: Liturgy Training Publications, 2016).

Living the Mass. Fr. Dom Grassi and Joe Paprocki (Chicago: Loyola Press, 2011).

Preparing Masses with Children: 15 Easy Steps. Robert W. Piercy, Jr. (Chicago: Liturgy Training Publications, 2012).

With Burning Hearts: A Meditation on the Eucharistic Life. Fr. Henri Nouwen (Maryknoll, NY: Orbis, 2016).

9

Parents and Evangelization

The Centrality of Evangelizing Households

If you don't mind, please read the following sentence twice. *Faith-formation ministry needs to be not so much about catechizing children as about evangelizing households.* This sentence is the best thesis statement I can offer for the state of faith formation in our time as it relates to children and families. Was there ever a time when Catholic parents knew their faith, loved their faith, lived their faith, and passed it on brilliantly to their children? I'm not sure. There remains the nostalgia that paints a picture of a bygone era (circa 1950s) as some kind of a Catholic utopia. At the same time, however, data continue to tell us in no uncertain terms that we are going in the wrong direction.

Catholic parents, as a whole, are less engaged in Catholic faith practice than in previous generations and the trend is likely to continue. This fact should make working with parents, if you are a catechetical leader of child faith-formation programming, your top priority. Gone are the days (if they actually ever existed) when a parish religious-education program or Catholic school could do its job and then hand the child back to the parents, safe in the knowledge that the family was praying together, talking about faith, living with Christ at the center of their lives, and, of course, going to Mass regularly.

A certain portion of your families are, of course, evangelized and active in their Catholic faith life. Don't forget about them, as they need and deserve to experience a substantive, flourishing catechesis that will enrich their faith. Even the strong flames of the evangelized need to be fanned in your parish. And more so, we can and should enlist such parents and other adults in witnessing to and teaching others. They can be leaven for the community.

A Shift of Mind-Set

Far too many families are not actively practicing their Catholic faith. Any veteran catechetical leader or pastor will rightly raise the concern, *How many of the families that just celebrated first Eucharist or confirmation are present the next weekend at Mass?* Try doing a count, and most likely it will be a stunning disappointment.

So what are we to do about this reality? In our increasingly secular, postmodern world it's become quite apparent that catechetical leadership, indeed, the entire parish, needs a change in thinking. We need to shift our mind-set

- *from* parish religious education (and Catholic school) primarily existing to teach information and dispense sacraments
- *to,* first and foremost, evangelization of families (which will include a kerygmatic, or core, formation offered in the context of personal witness).

Please note that this paradigm shift is not, ultimately, just about getting parents to value their children's faith more deeply. It's about getting parents to experience Catholic faith more deeply—in *themselves*!

Case Study: First Reconciliation Preparation

Parishes are diligent about preparing children for first reconciliation, and increasingly parishes are involving the parents in their child's formation. (In general, both in grade-level texts and in sacrament prep books, increasingly helpful sections are dedicated to parents so that they can learn and share with their child.) The goal, regarding preparation for first reconciliation, would seem to be making sure the child understands the sacrament, is able to make a smooth confession and have a positive experience, and develops the practice of regular confession. Of course, all these are worthwhile and important outcomes. But I humbly submit that there is a foundational goal here that is far larger than the aforementioned: to help both children and parents encounter the living Christ in their lives as the God who loves, heals, and saves them.

And of the two (child and parents), I'm *far* more interested in bringing the parents into a personal awakening to the divine love and mercy available to them in Christ. Think about it. If we return children to homes where their parent(s) have come to know Jesus and experience this relationship as saving good news in their lives, isn't there now real hope that the same will occur for them?

The child-only or child-first approach to which we are accustomed makes sense *within* a context of a vibrant and active faith being lived out in the family and parish. However, we are far from that reality. As daunting as it may seem, catechetical leaders of child programs have both parents *and* children to attend to—not merely to catechize but first to evangelize. We have a two-generation task before us.

Catechesis and Evangelization

I want to offer a quick analogy about the difference between catechesis and evangelization. *Evangelization* is like falling in love. There is the introduction, the getting to know, the deepening of relationship to the point of making a life commitment. Of course, we are called to fall in love with God, embodied and revealed in Jesus. Anyone who has been married knows that the hard work of maintaining and deepening a spousal relationship doesn't end on the wedding day: it begins! *Catechesis* is like the work a married couple engages in to enter ever more richly into the living mystery of their relationship. It is the beautiful work of a lifetime, and it's more about journey than destination. So it is, or can be, with God.

Let's drill down a bit on what evangelizing catechesis for parents might look like for first reconciliation preparation. We want parents to fully understand the following:

- They are loved by God, a personal and interested God.
- God is more powerful than evil and sin, including *their* sin.
- They are (as we all are) wounded, broken, and sinful and in need of God's mercy.
- God's merciful love is freely available, no matter the sin.
- Freedom, joy, and authenticity can mark our life in Christ.
- The sacrament of reconciliation is a powerful conduit of grace to heal their brokenness.
- The sacrament of reconciliation is a gift for a lifetime . . . for them and for their children.

Notice that the aim is far deeper than making sure that they help their child prepare for confession or go to the sacrament of reconciliation that first time with their child. It is even beyond inviting them to make the sacrament a part of their family's faith practice. All of that is there, implicitly and explicitly. But the underlying goal is to foster conversion in the parents to Jesus Christ broadly and personally and then as it relates to his loving mercy in the sacrament of reconciliation.

Sacraments on the Decline

I'd be rich (or at least modestly well-to-do) if I had a dollar for every time I've heard the following sentiment from parish catechetical leaders: "All these parents want is the sacrament [a.k.a. first communion]." I call it the "sacramental hit-and-run syndrome," and it's the bane of many catechetical leaders' ministry. It is deeply frustrating to plan so much, teach so much, care so much, and nonetheless watch families graduate out after the reception of a sacrament, often never to be seen or heard from again. Catholic sociologists have been fascinated over the years with the attraction to (or *stickiness of,* as some like to say) the sacraments. What draws people to present their child for sacraments when there may be little or no faith behind the motivation? Perhaps it is moral obligation or family pressure. Such "light" motivations, however, are having less sway with each passing generation.

The rate of reception of sacraments has been in significant decline in the last generation or two. According to the Center for Applied Research in the Apostolate (CARA), between 2000 and 2012, Church weddings decreased by approximately 40 percent, adult baptisms decreased by nearly 50 percent, infant baptisms decreased by 30 percent, and first communions decreased by 15 percent. The "stickiness" is breaking down. The bottom line is that we need to take a long, hard look at how Catholic parishes and faith-formation programs and schools are complicit in this erosion of faith practice, not in order to lay blame but rather to deal with the side of the equation that we can do something about.

Case Study: Baptism as Sacrament Hoop-Jumping . . . No More!

Back in the day when I was a parish catechetical leader, I noticed that many parents seeking baptism for their child were, more often than not, marginally tethered to or disconnected from the Catholic faith. It became apparent that baptismal-prep ministry was more an evangelizing opportunity than a catechizing ministry. As time passes, this only becomes truer. We must make the shift in our minds to view baptism ministry as evangelization primarily, and then develop and execute a plan accordingly.

Some parishes have turned the corner in this regard. They are, at least, asking the right questions about how to build evangelizing baptism ministry. We still have a distressingly long way to go. Too many parishes still function out of the erroneous presumption that parents coming to have their child baptized are largely evangelized and active Catholic people.

Catholicism has a profound theology of baptism. In our faith, baptism is so powerfully important: it is the key that unlocks everything else. Baptism has beautiful multilayered meaning and symbolism. For all our grand theology, it seems that our pastoral, formational, and liturgical approach to baptism is too often thin and vapid. Without a doubt, baptismal preparation has largely been our greatest evangelization opportunity squandered.

I like to say that the "cement is wet" at baptism and that by confirmation (and even first Eucharist) the cement of family faith identity and practice has greatly or fully hardened. Of course, this means that we have a far greater chance to make a difference in the faith practice and identity of a family at baptism than if we allow them to settle into an unevangelized lifestyle as a family for many years . . . and then attempt to write Jesus on their hearts at confirmation time, when the "cement" has long since dried.

My strong exhortation for parishes today is to *front-load* their efforts at impacting family systems. There is much more proverbial bang for the buck in doing front-loaded, *early* family evangelization ministry than anything later down the road! From my experience, baptismal ministry gets next-to-nothing in parish budgets and no staffing to speak of and barely registers on the landscape of parish ministries. This is stunningly myopic in an era when evangelization is so desperately needed and increasingly invoked. Whether or not you are charged with overseeing the baptismal ministry in your parish, be an advocate for this mind-set shift among parish leaders: the most important ministry for renewal in the life of a parish is baptismal ministry with follow-up opportunities that invite parents to learn Catholic/Christian parenting skills between baptism and first Eucharist.

The more you can front-load your evangelizing efforts to families when they are first establishing their patterns and practices, the greater the impact. Here are some practical suggestions for building an evangelizing baptismal ministry.

1. *Design every aspect of this ministry upon this primary principle and with great intentionality.* Baptism opens a wide window of opportunity to evangelize. See the window for baptismal ministry as open from the parents' inquiry to the child's sixth birthday! (Yes, you read that right!)

2. *Focus on team building and team formation.* There are many gifts present in the people of your parish and many and varied roles on any baptismal ministry team. Find your gifted people, form them well, and put them to work evangelizing. (Examples: A single mother on the team should help the ministry be sensitive to the needs of new single moms. You'll want people gifted in small-group facilitation. Identify parishioners gifted with being able to share their own faith journeys in ways that will resonate with these parents. Identify people who can be responsible for hospitality and creature comforts, including refreshments.)

3. *Build different tracks.* There should be one track for first-time parents and at least one different track for others. For example, one track might focus more on core elements of our faith and the baptismal rite, another one more on Catholic parenting and what the parish has to offer the family. However, any track should include a eucharistic focus and should seek to foster relationships within the community.

   And, tracks should consist of more than one session. (Don't be afraid of this. Let's not sell our faith short for the sake of expediency. The evangelization journey doesn't resemble a "path of least resistance.")

4. *Never call them classes or meetings.* Create more of a *day of formation/retreat* experience and frame it as such. Mix in strong relational interactions with some time for reflective quiet. Start any formational piece at the place of their lived experience and provide a core, kerygmatic message of Catholic faith that can speak to their lives as relevant *Good News*. Don't skimp on the hospitality and humor. Our joy in Christ should naturally radiate. (Who in your parish can witness with a joy that radiates and attracts?) There should be an exuberant sense of celebration in the preparation process, both for the gift of life in the child and in the gift of eternal life available in the sacrament.

5. *Give families an absolutely tremendous experience of baptism itself.* Let the sacrament and the community evangelize! This is done far more effectively within the context of Sunday Mass. Extravagant hospitality and joy should mark the posture of the parish throughout.

6. *Develop follow-up ministry for families between baptism and the school years.* There are countless ways to accomplish this, such as having regular and outreaching communication, creating a mentoring family relationship, and growing a ministry for mothers. (*Moms Ministry* is rich soil for bonding young families to a parish!) These are the key years that will help to determine what kind of relationship the family will ultimately have with your parish and with the Church.

Parents in Formation *with* Children

The focus of this chapter has been on parents and the need to create an environment in the parish that supports and fosters *their* conversion of faith to Christ Jesus. With this still as our larger goal, let's look at some

practical ways you can relate to parents and partner with them in the
faith development of their children.

1. Empower parents to a) lead family prayer and develop family
   faith practices, b) talk about God (Jesus) and share faith, and
   c) do service as a family. Encourage and reinforce these three vital
   dimensions for child faith development, and affirm parents in
   their ability to lead and form their children through these
   actions. (Example: As Hispanic families often model, parents can
   and should bless their children in words and gestures. This can
   be a powerful experience of love and security conveyed from
   parent to child, on behalf of God. Form families to embrace
   Catholic practices such as this in the home.)

2. Encourage parents to actively participate in the child's learning
   through parish faith formation. Create a culture of expectation
   for families to review and discuss the family learning page(s) each
   week. Try to steer this expectation away from mere homework
   drudgery toward high-quality family time with learning attached.
   (Parents will learn along with their children.)

3. Resource (to evangelize and catechize) parents in the digital
   world, where they live, on their computer and smartphone.
   Through e-mail, Facebook, Twitter, and next-generation
   technologies, feed them short snippets of good Catholic content
   to guide them in their prayer, in their understanding and
   articulation of Catholic faith, and in their role as primary
   catechists. Be generous in your use of video clips.

4. Resource parents beyond strictly faith themes. Our goal is always
   to demonstrate how life and faith can be intimately interwoven.
   Learn what are the greatest challenges and needs of parents and
   families today. Then provide resourcing assistance with an
   intentional faith spin to it (which you may have to insert
   yourself). This helps break down the artificial barrier between

"life" and "faith"—a barrier that makes it easier to dismiss Catholicism as irrelevant. And it will offer parents some very real value-added teaching from their parish in areas that could bless their lives, including finances, addiction, parenting, health, and relationships.

5. Weave into the matrix of family formation offerings, especially in the early grades, some parent coaching sessions. This can give parents hands-on guidance and practice in being the primary faith catechist for their child. These are highly practical sessions where the catechetical leader talks parents through activities and discussion in a specific, directive manner, to enable parents to become more comfortable with their role. (www.pastoral.center has a rich array of resources in parent coaching and many other aspects of family formation ministry.)

6. Create family tote bags with a set of materials designed for family prayer, discussion, and games. The materials for family use can include

   • liturgical-color cloth
   • crucifix, cross, image of Jesus
   • holy water
   • family faith game
   • conversation-starter cards
   • faith journal for the week
   • resources for family (DVD, CD, booklet)
   • resources for parents (book on Catholic spirituality, the Mass, basic teachings, etc.)

7. Invite (and yes, require) families to participate in some aspects of the life of the parish. Build into your program a joyful expectation of engagement in the parish. Create a menu of happenings in the parish, and ask them (at the start of the year)

to select the ones they will commit to doing as a family. This will help them get it on their calendars early. Examples: seasonal liturgies and devotions (stations of the cross), celebrations (Hispanic Las Posadas or Filipino Simbang Gabi or parish picnic), formational events (parish mission), or service opportunities (food-pantry collection or nursing-home visitation).

8. Offer adult faith-formation experiences during religious-education sessions. Invite (and keep inviting!) parents to join together for one or more modes of learning and sharing faith. Some will prefer watching a video series with a little discussion afterwards. Others may prefer a Lectionary-based faith-sharing group. Provide hospitality and an adult catechist to facilitate a group, and then see what happens. It may be slow to gain traction, but that's okay. Stay the course. Those who participate will benefit from it and may tell their friends. Don't be afraid to open this up to parishioners as a whole (unless that will scare off the parents).

This is certainly not an exhaustive list, even as you might be exhausted by just these possibilities. However, my hope is that it offers you a vision of the landscape upon which you can create *your own* set of modes and means for a) fostering conversion in parents, and b) assisting them in their role of bringing their children to a living and vibrant Catholic faith. Just remember that in this age, the latter without the former doesn't work and is contributing to the steep decline being experienced in our Church. Let's stop asking parents to give what they (in too many instances) do not have.

Raising Expectations

I sometimes wonder how a Church born on Pentecost can be so timid. Why do we leave the low-hanging fruit of Catholic parents (in RE programs *and* Catholic schools) so untouched, failing to vigorously engage them in pursuit of their conversion? I can only find three reasons.

1. lack of imagination
2. lack of missionary zeal
3. fear

Knowing that the Holy Spirit is with us, we should have no reason to fear! I offer a straightforward two-step game plan for parishes to consider.

1. Raise the expectations placed on parents and families.
2. Whatever you ask of them, make sure it will be a worthwhile experience for them.

Do not fear the inevitable resistance that will accompany such a plan. Christ Jesus calls us to boldness and gives us the Holy Spirit to strengthen us. The only real danger is maintaining the status quo.

Summary: Who Is Bringing the Children?

When he had finished speaking, he said to Simon, "Put out into the deep and let down your nets for a catch." (Luke 5:4)

Most parents today are candidates for some degree of evangelization, which looks and feels different from ongoing catechesis of intentional disciples of Jesus. Let's provide formation that invites their adult conversion and equips them with the spiritual/theological resources to take the lead in their children's formation. The opportunity for an abundant catch is there for the Church, and for your parish! Just be sure to give prime emphasis to baptismal ministry and the early years of the family cycle.

For Reflection and Discussion

- Are you in charge of adult faith formation in the parish? Even if not, you are helping form many adults—your parents! How do you collaborate with other adult-formation leaders in the parish to assist in this effort?

- Do parents today believe their way into belonging or belong their way into believing? Is parent ministry built to support both paths to life in Christ and to his Body, the Church?

Growing as a Catechetical Leader

Your ministry is increasingly shifting to an emphasis on *evangelization*. What skills and knowledge can you acquire to become an evangelization leader, to complement your role as a catechetical leader? If you want to evangelize parents, be sure to understand who they are—their hopes and fears, their interests and perspectives.

Go to www.loyolapress.com/ECL to access the worksheet.

Suggested Action

Consider what portion of parent meetings in your parish are directed to parents' heads. Plan the next session with at least half of the experience being directed to their hearts. Find and invite some parents and/or others to give inspiring (but relatable) witness to their own experience of faith.

For Further Consideration

Becoming a Parish of Intentional Disciples. Sherry A. Weddell, ed. (Huntington, IN: Our Sunday Visitor, 2015).

Faithful Families: Creating Sacred Moments at Home. Traci Smith (St. Louis, MO: Chalice Press, 2017).

Familiaris Consortio (The Role of the Christian Family in the Modern World). Pope Saint John Paul II (Boston: Pauline Books and Media, 2015).

Forming Families in Faith: Cultivating Catechesis in the Home. Kathy Hendricks (New London, CT: Twenty-Third Publications, 2015).

Forming Intentional Disciples: The Path to Knowing and Following Jesus. Sherry Weddell (Huntington, IN: Our Sunday Visitor, 2012).

Great Expectations: A Pastoral Guide for Partnering with Parents. Bill Huebsch (New London, CT: Twenty-Third Publications, 2010).

Infant Baptism: A Sourcebook for Parishes (Chicago: Loyola Press).

Keep Your Kids Catholic. Marc Cardaronella (Notre Dame, IN: Ave Maria Press, 2016).

Raising Faith-Filled Kids. Tom McGrath (Chicago: Loyola Press, 2000).

Sharing the Faith with Your Child: From Birth to Age Four. Phyllis Chandler, Joan Burney, and Mary Kay Leatherman (Liguori, MO: Liguori Publications, 2006).

You Have Put on Christ: Cultivating a Baptismal Spirituality. Jerry Galipeau (Franklin Park, IL: World Library Publications, 2014).

10

Mentoring the Next
Generation of Leaders

The Word Should Go On

My work on this book coincided with the first months of life for my first child, Daniel Thomas. As Kristi and I have watched our little guy grow and change, I see things from a radically new perspective. I like to joke, "Where did all the babies come from?" They weren't really on my radar before, and now I see them all over the place!

Not long ago I was introduced to the quote attributed to poet Carl Sandburg: "A baby is God's opinion that the world should go on." It is a wonderfully optimistic way of seeing life and of being invested in the future. To be in catechetical leadership, whether we have children or not, is to care passionately that each successive generation will know Jesus Christ, the Good News he embodied, and the mission he commissioned to us. Indeed, the *Word* should go on.

We are mere stewards of the Word of God, of the teachings and traditions of Catholic faith. For this time and in our respective places, we are called to carry out and share the graces given to us by God and the Church. We are yet another link in the two-millennium chain of stewards and faithful disciples of Jesus, seeking to ensure that Danny Quinlan and every other child born of this generation will know God, will love Jesus, and will live in Easter joy in this life and eternally.

Let's see the horizon, not only for next year and how God is calling *us* to lead but also to see the giftedness of people *around* us and for the years ahead. Let's look for whom God may be calling us to form into the next generation of catechetical leaders. I will be counting on your successor to oversee Spirit-led, grace-filled parish formation that may help Danny's children know Christ and live out their journeys as Catholic people.

Where We Are Going

Try looking ahead to the next twenty years. What do you see? Or, perhaps easier, go back twenty years and then imagine today. The world has changed so very much in two decades, has it not? Just with regard to ministry, I remember being a catechetical leader at a time when a personal computer was still only a dream for most people. My assistants had computers for managing data, but I didn't even own one! Now, in my diocesan ministry I couldn't accomplish a fraction of what I do without a computer and Internet connection. Technology has been a true revolution and vastly for the good in our ministry work.

Prognosticating is a dicey business. Even the wildest imagination might fail to see some of the big developments coming down the road. But any future vision related to catechetical ministry must be forged in the dynamic, ongoing interplay between the Church and the world, which reveals values and truths we can count on.

1. Evangelization and catechesis must always have as their end the person of Jesus Christ, the Word Incarnate, who reveals and embodies the love and saving power of the Father.
2. Catholic ministry is, in its essence, relational . . . human-divine and human-human.
3. The *story* (as modeled by Jesus) will always be primary in capturing the human religious imagination.

4. Leadership matters . . . educated, competent, faith-filled people called by God to serve Christ's mission.

5. Technology, where it can be a friend to ministry and further Christ's mission, must be embraced.

6. Cultural trends must be discerned with both openness and guardedness for compatibility with the Church's mission.

7. The Holy Spirit needs to be in charge, which requires leaders to stay flexible, humble, and spiritually attuned.

The Church: An Enduring Sacrament Engaging the World

I love working for the Church. Those of us who do so have the best of both worlds—a ground beneath us that is unshakeable and the breath of the Holy Spirit blowing winds of change through the Church and the world. Our Church, called to be confident, doesn't tend to swerve all over the place. Our Church, called to be humble, must stay open to the surprises of God, as Pope Francis has often said. We have a body of truth that is timeless and divinely revealed and that creates a cohesive framework for the Catholic worldview. While so much of the landscape of our world is in radical upheaval and entire systems are at risk of being overturned, the Catholic system of thought holds steady and true over the unfolding span of history. It has weathered centuries of upheaval and threat and has come through it all.

One of the reasons Catholicism has survived and thrived in its two millennia is precisely because it has had a genius for innovation and adaptation along the way. From its history of missionary inculturation of the faith to our recent popes' embrace of the Internet as a tool for evangelization, where the Church has been flexible and embracive, it has furthered the mission of Christ. The Church is at its best when it holds the tension between *already* and *not yet* (like Jesus' explanation of the reign of God in the Gospels). This is a theological concept that proposes a mode of being for the Church. Catholicism is strong enough, flexible enough, and so utterly brilliant a system of thought to be able to reject 1) fundamentalism (which denies complexity and ridicules nuance) and 2) relativism (which flattens truth and reason in the name of tolerance) at the same time. Both are deadly to the organic unfolding of the Church as the living, breathing, evolving sacrament of Jesus Christ. Both endanger the Church—relativism more from our culture, fundamentalism more from within.

How wonderful to serve something so big, so great, so true! We participate in the mystery of divine love and grace, which climaxed in the person of Jesus Christ and continues to dynamically unfold to this very day in our world, in your life and in mine. Within this context, we transmit truths that are eternal and salvific, transcendent of temporal influence, and not subject to the tyranny of cultural insistence. The Catholic faith gives us both roots and wings for sound, enduring catechetical leadership.

So, bring on the future. As Catholic catechetical leaders, we have full confidence in what God is bringing about in our time and beyond. We are agents of Christ's Good News and the Catholic worldview, a fullness of truth beyond any other human construct. And we receive the flow of constant change undaunted and with joy, spying always the potential for proclaiming Christ Jesus anew. Indeed, the future will continue to offer us new wineskins for the most precious gift that is Christ's Gospel. And, by the grace of God, we will be ready!

Influencing Future Servant-Leaders

"You're not allowed to leave until you find your replacement." I've heard this line in different ministry settings over the years, and I've actually used it myself. It's a good one-liner, and you might be tempted to use it on your catechists. You'll get some laughs, as long as they know you are half-joking. Perhaps the most important future-oriented responsibility of a catechetical leader is to invite others to enter into ministry and possibly into ministry leadership. A good leader is one who continually looks to share responsibilities and foster growth in others. One who possesses real *authority* is one who helps others reach their potential.

Think back over your journey of life and faith. Consider the path that brought you to the place you are now. It certainly is a journey of grace. It probably has surprising twists and turns. Very few of you, I suspect, grew up wanting to be parish catechetical leaders. I'm sure you can think of key people in your past, people you would consider agents of God, who drew you forward on the ministerial path and helped you to recognize your own giftedness. Most of us have one or more people to thank (or blame, on our worst days) for bringing us into catechetical leadership, even though at first we may have been unsure about what exactly God was calling us to.

When I look back, I can see the way God used many people to form me and guide me in my vocation as a catechetical leader. Retrospection is a lot easier than forecasting, isn't it? As my wise friend and colleague Dr. Jim Healy puts it, "The road straightens out behind us." Here are some of the people God used to nudge and nurture me into catechetical leadership.

- The associate pastor who took time to counsel me and pointed me to the DRE
- The DRE who gave an eighteen-year-old a chance and the formation to grow
- The spiritual director who gave me hope and direction as I was leaving the seminary
- The diocesan catechetical staff person who invited me to apply for parish positions
- The neighboring DRE who mentored me in my first years
- Parishioners who were patient and affirming of the rookie

- The deanery group who stretched me and provided a sense of community
- The diocesan director who believed in me enough to invite me onto her staff
- The diocesan committee who recommended me for the director position

These are just a few of the folks who had a hand in shaping my path for catechetical leadership. I owe so many people so much! It does indeed "take a village" to form any of us for leadership in the Church. Reflecting on this inspires me to "pay it forward" and help others achieve all that God is calling them to. This is my responsibility and my joyful privilege.

Spend some time creating your list of key mentors and supporters. I also encourage you to take some meaningful time, when you can, to reflect upon the grace-filled and unique journey you have traveled in response to God's mysterious call to lead and serve. Go back now and again to interpret and celebrate how God has led you and how you have responded. And thank God for those who helped you along the way. Maybe thank them, too.

Charisms and Talents

There has been a lot of talk in the Church in recent years about the giftedness of each baptized person. This is a valuable reclamation of the early church's understanding that God blesses every member of the body of Christ with spiritual gifts (charisms) to strengthen the community. In *Forming Intentional Disciples*, Sherry Weddell speaks about charisms as Spirit-given gifts that have only one purpose: to bless others in the name of Christ Jesus. The StrengthsFinder assessment tool, published by Gallup, is one example of an assessment tool that can show you the human strengths that are apparent in you for leadership.

Over the years I've suggested that being a parish catechetical leader is to be, among many things, a leadership *talent scout*, or perhaps I should say a *charism scout*. One of your responsibilities as a catechetical leader is to be on the lookout for people with both natural talents and supernatural charisms.

Calling out talents and charisms is not the same as filling empty slots in ministry. Be respectful of and attentive to the movement of the Holy Spirit in your parish. Be *person*-centered as you discern whom to invite forward into ministry leadership roles, and be open to creating ministries that fit the talents and charisms of certain individuals God has provided.

Grounding Everything in Prayer

The starting point for this work of calling out the gifts of others is prayer. You are called to be in regular prayer for those you currently shepherd in ministerial roles and as future leaders. Ask God to call new people into ministry roles. Ask for the grace to perceive the charisms and talents of parishioners. Ask God to open hearts and minds of parishioners to this call to grow and serve.

Endeavor to make this a prayer campaign beyond yourself. Invite catechists, staff colleagues, parents, and others into an active and intentional calling down the Holy Spirit to activate the gifts present in the baptized of the community. There is evidence that parishes that pray with this intentionality experience renewal more dramatically.

People-First Leadership

Get to know your people. This is critical in being able to perceive the giftedness inherent in your parish. Take time to listen, observe, and learn. Look for pastoral gifts, teaching gifts, leadership gifts. Scout parents and other adults who are perhaps not currently in active ministries. Often some of the brightest gems are not in ministry, for any

number of reasons. Also, be attentive to those currently in other ministerial roles. Some may not be suited to their current ministry position.
Some may actually thrive and serve more effectively in a different role.
Using this approach to ministry matchmaking, you start with the person and his or her gifts and then try to find an optimal avenue for
tapping into the person's talents and charisms.

While matching the gifts of parishioners to the needs of the parish
community may seem obvious, it can be difficult to adhere to. When
you have five junior high catechist slots to fill and it is August, you'll be
tempted to see everyone as a natural with seventh-graders. Be careful.
A ministry mismatch will often result in unhappy catechists doing an
ineffectual job and leaving in January. Avoid having a utilitarian view
of people. The intuitive and respectful catechetical leader will value
persons in their own right and not as corks to plug a hole. This may
result in an imbalance on the ministry landscape in the short-term.
However, this Spirit-led approach will allow new and life-giving ministries to begin, others to die as God may intend, and parishioners to
be more fulfilled in serving according to their strengths and charisms
more than according to parish needs.

My Favorite Mentoring Story

My greatest success as a DRE parish talent scout was Marie. Marie had
four boys in our RE program. She was an engaged Catholic parent and
seemed to be a joyful, faith-filled woman. I related to her for a couple
of years and wondered why she wasn't a catechist. Over time I got to
know Marie and gained a sense of where her giftedness lay. One day
I felt inspired to talk to Marie about the new Children's Catechumenate Ministry we were starting the following year. As I explained the
role, she became excited and eager to be a part of the team. Her talents and charisms were a perfect fit for the role, and she soon became

lead catechist with the children. In time, I handed the ministry over to Marie. Her ministry in this role was fruitful, and she was deeply joyful.

Having seen leadership potential in Marie, I tried to train her both as a catechist for the ministry and as ministry coordinator. Eventually, Marie went on to get her undergraduate and master's degrees and became a long-standing, valuable member of the parish staff. I'd like to think that when I left my parish position, it was okay because I had found a replacement, someone more capable and gifted than I to carry on.

Empowering Others for Leadership

The Church has a tremendous need for members of the baptized to continue to enter into catechetical leadership. If God is, indeed, calling a sufficient (and perhaps an abundant) number of people, we need to become talent/charism scouts and also vocation directors, not only helping people to see their giftedness but also guiding them to build up their skills. An effective catechetical leader is one who naturally mentors those called by God and gifted for leadership. Here are ten ways to mentor potential future catechetical leaders:

1. Affirm them—not just what they do but also *who* they are.

2. Invite them to consider suitable roles in ministry, including starting new ministries (possibly ones that they discover).

3. If leadership is apparent, offer opportunities to step into roles of greater responsibility over time.

4. Accompany them (being available to provide counsel and support), and invite them to accompany you (shadowing you in your role to learn more firsthand).

5. Pray for those you are mentoring in a more intensive way, and pray for yourself in your vital role.

6. Prayerfully conduct theological reflection together in light of their ministry leadership experiences.

7. Mutually assess their areas of strength and of needed growth.

8. Explore formation and education opportunities to further their ministry leadership competency.

9. Continue to empower them with greater freedom to lead and create in their leadership roles.

10. Consult your diocesan catechetical office for resources available to assist in the process.

Valuing Competent Catechetical Leadership

Increasingly, people are being thrust into positions of catechetical leadership without the proper formation and the training they deserve. There are a number of factors involved in this growing dynamic. One is that there are fewer people with the education, experience, and training to serve as catechetical leaders. This is a systemic issue, not dissimilar to the shortage we see in the priesthood. Another obvious reason is that some parishes seek to staff catechetical leadership at a reduced cost to the parish. Simply put, people with less education and experience tend to be paid less. A parish may take this approach due to a lack of financial resources or due to a lack of valuing catechesis.

In response, I urge you to advocate for an appreciation in your parish that faith formation is a foundational ministry to the evangelizing mission of Christ, which is why it is also a canonical obligation. It is at the heart of what a parish is called to be, and the mission of Christ demands that we invest for excellence in each generation. So much is at stake here!

Opportunities to Grow

As you mentor others into leadership roles, don't shy away from the possibility that they pursue formal education. Catechetical leaders must have some level of theological command. It simply isn't good enough that they have good hearts and a love for Jesus and the Catholic faith. Formal education can mean working to achieve a certificate or a degree from a Catholic college or university. For those interested in making their living in catechetical leadership, this should be the preferred option, even if it may take several years to complete.

Fortunately, bachelor's degrees and advanced degrees in religious education or other related fields are more accessible now than ever, thanks to online learning. Similarly, there are online certificate tracks offered through many Catholic institutions (universities and others). These certificate tracks can be a portal into more formal studies and can often naturally allow one to transition into a degreed program.

There is little reason today for someone growing into catechetical leadership not to pursue, in the classroom or online (or in a blended approach), the needed formal education to lead with formal competency. This path is available to all, and the parish, diocese, and university can (and should) do much to make sure that the cost remains within reason.

Your diocesan catechetical office should be a great resource for anyone wishing to further his or her education and develop these core competencies for ministry leadership. Be sure to consult with your diocesan leadership. Check to see if there are diocesan funding avenues for leadership development. Challenge those in whom you see potential to strive for greatness. The Church needs gifted people who grow to their full potential to deliver outstanding leadership. This applies to both you and those whom you mentor.

National Standards and Competencies

Key national Catholic ministry associations (including the National Conference for Catechetical Leadership [NCCL], National Federation for Catholic Youth Ministry [NFCYM], and National Association for

Lay Ministry) have jointly developed a helpful set of standards that any catechetical leader should review. These standards and their related core competencies can be a measure of one's preparedness and ability to serve effectively as a catechetical leader (or other ministry leader) in the Church. I encourage you to visit www.nccl.org to explore the *Certification Standards for Lay Ecclesial Ministers: Standards and Competencies*. These standards can be helpful as you develop your plan for continuing professional and personal growth and can help others explore their path into catechetical leadership.

Mentoring for Challenge: Failure and Critique

A good mentor puts one in a position to succeed more often than not. However, growth comes more notably from our experiences of challenge than from our successes. So, allow those you mentor to stretch their wings, try things beyond their comfort zone, and possibly fail. It is all a part of the learning curve. The important thing will be how they deal with difficulties. Be ready to coach them; better yet, model for them the fortitude, humility, and flexibility required for catechetical leadership. Share from your own challenging experiences. Be transparent and even vulnerable with those you seek to mentor.

Also, don't be afraid to challenge them regarding their areas for growth. Within a relationship of trust, a good mentor can be honest and name what needs improvement. Such honesty and accountability are actually generous and loving. But remember that we need to be affirmed ten times for every criticism. So don't miss an opportunity to celebrate successes and affirm growth.

Closing Thought

In response to God's lavish graciousness in my life and the remarkable generosity of spirit of so many from whom I've learned (and continue to learn), I feel an increasing obligation to share any wisdom and perspective I might now have. This book, which has been enriched greatly by the expertise of wonderful parish catechetical leaders in the Diocese of Joliet (including a former one, my wife) and other friends-colleagues, has been an attempt to do this.

Perhaps these are words that can resonate with you or inspire you as you live and lead:

> This is the true joy in life, the being used for a purpose recognized by yourself as a mighty one; the being a force of nature instead of a feverish, selfish little clod of ailments and grievances complaining that the world will not devote itself to making you happy.
>
> I am of the opinion that my life belongs to the whole community, and as long as I live it is my privilege to do for it whatever I can.
>
> I want to be thoroughly used up when I die, for the harder I work the more I live. I rejoice in life for its own sake. Life is no "brief candle" for me. It is a sort of splendid torch which I have got hold of for the moment, and I want to make it burn as brightly as possible before handing it on to future generations. (attributed to George Bernard Shaw)

Saint John of the Cross puts the whole of life's meaning in quite succinct, poetic terms: "In the evening of life you shall be judged by Love." For closing purposes on catechetical leadership, I offer you this: Live in God's love, and you will be able to love your people as Christ loves. The rest may not be easy . . . but it will make perfect sense.

Summary: An Advocate We Can Count On

He will give you another Advocate to be with you always, the Spirit of truth. (John 14:16–17, NABRE)

As Jesus looked ahead on the night before he died, he prayed for his disciples, and "not only for them, but also for those who will believe in me through their word" (John 17:20, NABRE). Jesus had mentored the apostles to continue his work and to mentor others into discipleship. Because his plan for the future depended upon human beings, he gave us the Holy Spirit. The Spirit continues to bestow charisms upon his people so that the word of God may go on.

For Reflection and Discussion

- Fundamentalism and relativism are dangers as we seek to hold the Gospel and the world in dynamic tension. Which of these is the greater risk in your parish? In yourself?

- The Holy Spirit is generous in giving parish communities talents and charisms, though many of them may remain unrecognized or not yet be placed at the service of the Church. How can you be a more attentive scout on behalf of the Spirit?

Growing as a Catechetical Leader

Ask people you trust to help you see areas of further growth potential for you. Explore a concrete step toward raising your competency in one (or more) areas for growth: a course, reading, skills training, etc.

Go to www.loyolapress.com/ECL to access the worksheet.

Suggested Action

Take some time to think of an individual you are mentoring in some way. Using the list on page 149, choose the elements you need to give greater attention to. Create a more intentional strategy for your mentorship of this person.

For Further Consideration

The Art of Mentoring: Embracing the Great Generational Transition. Darlene Zschech (Bloomington, MN: Bethany House Publishers, 2011).

Coaching in Ministry: How Busy Church Leaders Can Multiply Their Ministry Impact. Keith E. Webb (Bellevue, WA: Active Results LLC, 2015).

Everyone Leads: How to Revitalize the Catholic Church. Chris Lowney (Lanham, MD: Rowman & Littlefield, 2017).

The Elements of Mentoring. W. Brad Johnson and Charles R. Ridley (New York: St. Martin's Press, 2008).

The Heart of Mentoring. David A. Stoddard (Colorado Springs: NavPress, 2014).

StrengthsFinder 2.0. Tom Rath (New York: Gallup Press, 2007).

About the Author

Tom Quinlan was a parish DRE and has served as a diocesan cat-echetical director since 2001. He holds a Masters of Divinity from University of St. Mary of the Lake. Tom has been active in NCCL, including as a board member. A strong voice for *evangelizing catechesis*, Tom does conference presentations and consultation work across the country. He and his family live in the Chicago area.

The Effective Catechetical Leader Series

Whether you are starting out as a catechetical leader or have been serving as one for many years, **The Effective Catechetical Leader** series will help you use every aspect of this ministry to proclaim the Gospel and invite people to discipleship.

Called by Name
Preparing Yourself for the Vocation of Catechetical Leader

Catechetical Leadership
What It Should Look Like, How It Should Work, and Whom It Should Serve

Developing Disciples of Christ
Understanding the Critical Relationship between Catechesis and Evangelization

Cultivating Your Catechists
How to Recruit, Encourage, and Retain Successful Catechists

Excellence in Ministry
Best Practices for Successful Catechetical Leadership

All God's People
Effective Catechesis in a Diverse Church

Each book in **The Effective Catechetical Leader** series is available for $13.95, or the entire series is available for $65.00.

To Order:
Call **800.621.1008** or visit **loyolapress.com/ECL**

The ECL App

Everything You Need to Be an Effective Catechetical Leader

The ECL app puts wisdom and practical help at your fingertips. Drawn directly from the six books of **The Effective Catechetical Leader** series, ECL provides an opportunity for catechetical leaders to center themselves spiritually each day, focus on specific pastoral issues, and identify go-to strategies for meeting the challenges of serving as an effective catechetical leader.

Special Features:

- Over 40 unique guided reflections tailored to your individual pastoral ministry needs.
- On-the-go convenience and accessibility on your phone or tablet.
- Modern design, easy-to-use interface, and a source of calm amidst the busy schedule of a catechetical leader.

For more details and to download the app, visit
www.loyolapress.com/ECL